NOMINAL CHRISTIANITY

World Studies of Churches in Mission

NOMINAL CHRISTIANITY

Studies of Church and People in Hamburg

by

JUSTUS FREYTAG AND KENJI OZAKI

LONDON
LUTTERWORTH PRESS

First published 1970

COPYRIGHT © 1970 THE COMMISSION ON WORLD MISSION AND
EVANGELISM OF THE WORLD COUNCIL OF CHURCHES

Translated into English by Marjorie Sandle

ISBN 0 7188 1758 3

*Printed in Great Britain
by Ebenezer Baylis and Son Limited
The Trinity Press, Worcester, and London*

CONTENTS

EDITORIAL FOREWORD

WHEN this series was launched several years ago, it was conceived as 'a search to understand, at a deeper level than a general survey can attempt, what it means for individual Christians or local churches to stand at a particular point of time in a given situation; how do they respond to the different factors in this environment, and what influences and determines this response?' Among the various 'typical' situations to be investigated, it seemed desirable to include a study of what might be described, in hybrid fashion, as a *post-Volkskirchliche situation*, such as obtains in Germany and Scandinavia. Here Church and society have been so closely connected with one another in the past, and have yet been so subject to the influence of urbanization and secularization, that the majority of the people still call themselves Christian, yet now have little connection with the congregational life of the Church, though it remains an established institution in society.

After various enquiries, the town of Hamburg was selected for this particular study, and the services of two research workers were secured. Dr. Justus Freytag had already, at an early age, made a name for himself as a church sociologist. The Rev. Kenji Ozaki had come from Japan to serve in a Hamburg pastorate for three years, in order to gain for his church at home some knowledge of developments in the church life of the West. These two men have contributed the two parts of this study.

It was difficult at first to decide in which order to place these two reports. They are complementary one to the other. Mr. Ozaki has analysed the situation of a particular Hamburg congregation, from the vantage point of a pastor from another culture who had to adapt himself to life and work in modern Germany; he has further given some important indications as to the lines of reform he sees desirable. Dr. Justus Freytag, on the other hand, has been particularly concerned with Christians outside the organized Church. What is now the motivation and content of their 'latent Christianity'? This will demonstrate the mutual effect which Church and environment have had upon each other. Is the 'general', or 'nominal', Christianity found in such a situation still in any sense genuinely Christian? What should be the Church's role today? In the appendices, Dr. Freytag has described the sociological methods used to investigate these questions. It has finally been decided to place the latter study second, because to do otherwise might wrongly imply that Mr. Ozaki was attempting to give concrete answers to the questions which result from Dr. Freytag's research, whereas, in fact, Dr. Freytag has analysed the situation, and made many valuable observations, but has quite rightly—in terms of the briefing given to authors in this series—left readers in the main to seek their own answers and remedies to the situation revealed. Volumes in this series are simply designed to hold a mirror to the facts, and so to stimulate reflection and action.

We are very indebted to the Evangelical Academy in Hamburg for their permission to use the results of a research project originally carried through under their auspices, and subsequently written up by Dr. Freytag as a participant; to Bishop Hans-Otto Wölber of the Landeskirche Hamburg, for granting leave of absence to Dr. Freytag to carry out this study; and to Pastor Erich Ramsauer, Director of the Bremen Mission, for generously extending Mr. Ozaki's time in Hamburg, in order to enable him to undertake this particular task. We also thank the Rev. M. A. Halliwell for help in translating some of the material at an earlier stage, and Miss Marjorie Sandle for wrestling with translation of the complete manuscript.

Geneva   VICTOR E. W. HAYWARD
December 1969

A. A LOCAL CHURCH FACING ITS REFORM

by

Kenji Ozaki

AUTHOR'S PREFACE

THE following investigation depicts a metropolitan parish of the Hamburg Regional Church (*Hamburgische Landeskirche*), and is concerned with the problems of parish reform which have been raised in its core group. The main part of the report deals with a catalogue of questions which become significant at the point when the inner circle of the congregation begins to search for possible ways of renewing itself. An attempt is made to trace these questions back to their origins in the social structure of the congregation, and to their roots in the accepted norms of church life. This will show why they have such an urgency for the congregation under investigation. At the same time, it is hoped that this analysis of the situation may lead to the formulation of some initial, provisional steps to be undertaken, which could develop into a renewal of congregational life.

As an introduction to the main part of this report, a detailed statistical section is provided that conveys a broad idea of the sphere of influence of the congregation in its area, as well as a description of its location and history. The concluding section emphasizes the need for conscious membership in the Church, in light of the changed popular understanding of the relation between Church and State, as well as the growing realization that, as a Christian, one is in a minority, and the loosening of the connection between being a member of the congregation and being an inhabitant of the parish. The problems of the missionary outreach of the congregation under investigation are outlined against the background of the extensive changes which are taking place in the understanding of affiliation to the Church.

After serving for seven years as a pastor of the United Church of Christ in Japan, I was sent by my Church to work for three years within a Church in Europe. The report which follows is the result of two years' work as a pastor in the parish under investigation. Coming from a Church of another culture, I had, as an investigator, both a broader and at the same time a more limited perspective. Nevertheless I hope that the fact that I had to approach this assignment as an outsider has helped to give more validity to my observations.

Hamburg
1965

KENJI OZAKI

3

Survey of the Parish under Investigation

1. LOCATION AND HISTORY OF THE PARISH

THE PARISH under investigation is in a purely residential area, two or three kilometres from the centre of the city. A six-lane arterial highway runs through the middle of the parish to the eastern part of the town. The parish is connected with the city area by two Underground Railway stations along the main traffic artery and two City Railway stations at either end of the parish. The parish is bounded on the south by a railway line, on the west by a main thoroughfare, on the north by a canal, and on the east by a number of small roads. It is trapezium-shaped, with a base about a kilometre long, which is in fact the railway, and three other sides each 0·7 kms in length. The great majority of the houses in this area are four-story flats. The church, church hall and two parsonages lie in the southern part of the parish, not far from the underground and city railway stations, and are therefore easily accessible for members of the congregation who live outside the parish.

The first church organization in the parish dates from 1845. In that year a relatively new form of church activity, a Sunday School, was established, with 8 teachers and about 80 children. At that time about 500 people lived in the area of the present parish. Although the Sunday School was closed 14 years later, various lay people attempted during the following decade to restart the work. A growth in the number of inhabitants, due to an influx from the countryside, caused a new start to be made in 1872. At first this took the form of work with neglected children, and a children's home was founded by two young ladies with the support of the Church. Two years later the first church hall was built, which served at the same time as a chapel. In 1878 the first pastor was called to serve the parish. Four years later the congregation became self-supporting, and after seven years, in 1885, it had built and dedicated its own church. Meanwhile the number of inhabitants in the parish had increased to 10,000, and the old church hall was used as a second preaching place.

The second pastor, who began his work there in 1890, built up the congregation in a way which was an example for the whole town. His younger colleague, who was appointed to the second living created in 1896, wrote: 'His earnest concern was directed towards making the Christian congregation the place where all, rich and poor, high and low, employer and employee, could come together, because they all received the same love from God, and all were engaged in serving one another, in voluntary sharing and giving. Beneath the pulpit of this church a vast congregation soon gathered, from the parish and from the whole town of Hamburg.' The strong features of parish work at this time were the 'classical literature evening' for young people, the 'open evening' for adults, at which there was free conversation about all needs and complaints, the Women's Circle, the loan fund for members of the congregation who were in financial need, the welfare committee which, at that period of industrial change and concentration of population in the metropolis, investigated causes of distress and gave advice to those who were affected by them, and the congregational festival which united all members of the congregation once a year.

Before the First World War a further living was added, and in 1908 a new church hall was built. By this time 44,000 people lived in the parish. The speech delivered at the dedication of the church hall reveals how the congregation understood their task in the social struggles and internal disagreements in the Church between liberal and reformed theology. This hall was dedicated to serve the cause of personal peace, through witness to the strength imparted by belief in the crucified and risen Lord, through the power of a living experience of him. It was to serve the cause of ecclesiastical peace, for in it the will of God and brotherly love were to be practised. For it is only the doing of God's will and the practice of brotherly love that lead to a firmness of belief in which all sincere Christians can unite. The church hall was to contribute to peace in society, because within those places intended for the Church and congregation there is always the living hope that the whole population will rediscover the Gospel.

After the First World War, when the population had reached some 60,000, the parish was divided. In 1926 a new church was completed, around which a new parish with two pastors came into being.

During the National Socialist era the pastors of the congregation under investigation belonged to the Confessing Church. The situation of the congregation became difficult when, in 1941, one of the pastors died and was succeeded by a pastor who was associated with the German Christian Movement. This movement was composed of that wing of the Church which, generally speaking, sympathized with National Socialism. In this way a division was created in the congregation which, even after the death of National Socialism, had an inhibiting effect on the reconstruction of the congregation. In 1943 most of the houses in the parish were destroyed in air raids. The church, the church hall and one of the parsonages were bombed. In the neighbouring parish only the church remained, and in the parish under investigation, only one parsonage escaped destruction. At the end of the war, in 1946, only 5,000 people remained in the few houses not destroyed in the parish. In comparison with the neighbouring daughter parish, where the congregation was able after the war to meet in an undamaged church, the parish under investigation was faced with much greater problems in reconstruction. Services and meetings were held in the cellar of the parsonage, which was the only undamaged house in its neighbourhood.

The parish had disintegrated, not only because most of the parishioners had found accommodation in other parts of the town or outside it after the bombing, but also because violent disagreements between the pastors, which originated during the time of National Socialism, still persisted behind the scenes. After the old pastors had been moved to other parishes and many new blocks of flats were erected in the area in 1955, a new generation of pastors was able to combine forces with the congregation for the restoration of the church and church hall, which was completed in 1960.

Today two pastors work in the parish. They have the following full-time assistants: a lay deacon, a woman worker, a sister, an organist, the keeper of the parish registers, and a verger. The parish is run by the two pastors and an elected church council of twelve. The rebuilt church seats 350. In the newly-built church hall there is a kindergarten for 60 children, with two teachers. In 1961 the population of the parish was about 17,000.

2. DATA ABOUT THE SOCIAL STRUCTURE OF THE PARISH

(a) *Structure of the population and religious affiliation in the area*

Half of the working population are salaried employees. The population is divided as follows according to occupation:

	PARISH AREA	HAMBURG
Total number of employed persons	8,593	1,420,292
Self-employed	13%	11%
Members of the family who assist	3%	2%
Officials/civil servants	8%	8%
Salaried employees	47%	35%
Wage earners	24%	43%
Apprentices	5%	1%

(Data from the Regional Statistics Office, Hamburg: 1961 Census.)

Thus the parish lies in a middle-class district.

Every year about one fifth of the inhabitants of the parish move house. In the year 1963, 17% of the inhabitants moved away and 19% moved in (data from the District Office). The fact is significant for parish work, because it means that there is a certain mobile portion of the population with which it cannot keep in touch for any length of time. This limits the long-term work of the parish, which is concerned to build trust and friendship between the various families and the congregation.

Of the inhabitants, 76% are members of the Evangelical Lutheran Church. After this the next largest group is those who have left the Church or who do not belong to any Christian denomination. Then follow the members of the Roman Catholic Church.

2

PARISH AREA		CITY OF HAMBURG	
No. of inhabitants	17,151		1,832,346
Evang.-Lutheran	75·6%	Protestant	76·6%
Reformed	0·7%	Roman Catholic	7·4%
Free Church	0·8%	Jews	0·1%
Roman Catholic	7·0%	Others	15·9%
Others	15·9%		

(Data from the Regional Statistics Office, Hamburg: 1961 Census.)

A breakdown of the 'Others' according to streets indicates that the people who have no connection with the Christian faith live in the small working-class area and in the small villa-type area of the parish. Neither type of street is typical for the parish.

The number of those leaving the Church exceeds the number of those joining the Church, but in any case the numbers of those who leave, join or change confessions are very small. The statistics of those leaving the Church are recorded for church tax purposes at the Registry Office.

The statistics referred to below as Data A are for a period of one year, calculated from the average of a four-year period (1960–64) for four parishes with approximately the same population, the same number of members of the Evangelical Lutheran Church, similar residential areas, and the same number of people with a full-time occupation. (Source: Regional Church Office, Hamburg.)

The statistics referred to as Data B are for a period of one year, calculated from the average of a four-year period (1960–64) in the parish under survey. (Collected in the parish.)

The following are the data on religious behaviour in the area of Hamburg City or of the Hamburg Regional Church.

	PARISH AREA	HAMBURG REGIONAL CHURCH, 1961
Persons rejoining the Church	6	
Conversions from the Roman Catholic Church	2	
Adult Baptisms	5	
Total number of accessions in the year	13	769
Persons leaving the Church during the year	57	3,083
Persons leaving the Church as percentage of Ev.-Lutheran Church members (Data A)	0·4%	0·4%

(b) *Requests for the occasional offices of the Church*

Infant baptism and church funerals are the most important occasions for which the services of the Church are sought.

	PARISH AREA	CITY OF HAMBURG
Baptisms during the year	145	18,011
No. of baptisms as percentage of births where both parents are Ev.-Lutherans (Data A)		87·5%
Funerals during the year	70	14,985
Church funerals as percentage of deaths of Ev.-Lutherans (Data A)		81·7%

In contrast with the events of birth and death, in which man is most strongly conscious of the mercy or the inscrutability of the Creator, in the case of marriage the choice and decision of individuals are more prominent. A person must be personally responsible for the choice of partner and the planning of a marriage. Over and above that, a church marriage also involves particular social duties in regard to the celebration of the wedding day. For this reason only half the members of the Regional Church who are married ask for a church service, in addition to the obligatory civil ceremony.

	PARISH AREA	CITY OF HAMBURG
Weddings during the year	46	7,318
Church weddings as percentage of civil marriages where couples are both Ev.-Lutherans (Data A)		55·4%

Confirmation usually takes place at the age of 14. It comes at the end of two years of instruction from the pastor, which fill out and deepen the religious teaching given at school. At confirmation the young person is admitted to the Lord's Supper.

	PARISH AREA	CITY OF HAMBURG
Confirmations during the year (Data A)	141	16,102

Because of the shift of population and the varying birth-rates each year, it is impossible to ascertain what proportion of children baptized are later confirmed. Only some parents send their children to confirmation instruction. Among the confirmands, only a small number find their way to belief without parental encouragement. Most of the confirmands regard confirmation as a social custom. A certain percentage of children who take part in instruction and are confirmed do not come from purely Evangelical-Lutheran homes. In these cases one of the parents, most often the father, has left the Church or one of the parents belongs to another denomination. They comprise on an average 13% of those confirmed in the parish under investigation.

(c) *Attendances at services and participation in the Lord's Supper*

Though one may regard regular Sunday worship as the norm for a Christian way of life, yet only a very small proportion of Church members can be said to behave dutifully.

	PARISH AREA	HAMBURG REGIONAL CHURCH, 1961
No. of people attending church on Sunday (Average no. of attendances out of 4 Sundays in the year taken at random)	213	14,012
No. of people attending church on Sunday as percentage of the Ev.-Lutheran population (Data A)	1·6%	2·0%

The percentage of regular worshippers becomes higher if it is not assessed according to regular church-going every Sunday, but is divided into several different patterns of regular attendance. One can distinguish three groups of church-goers, each with individual habits as follows: (1) church-goers who come every Sunday; (2) those who come every second or third Sunday; (3) occasional worshippers who attend services about five times a year. According to the estimates, the congregation on a normal Sunday would be composed of: those who attend every week (30%), those who attend alternate weeks (60%), and occasional attenders (10%). The following tables give a picture of those who attend at all regularly.

	PARISH AREA
Those who participate in Sunday services with any regularity, as percentage of the Ev.-Lutheran population	4·2%

Since children up to 13 years old do not take part in the services, it is more appropriate to assess church attendance in relation to the

Evangelical-Lutheran population over 13 years old. Once again this can only be estimated.

PARISH AREA

Those who participate in Sunday services with any regularity, as percentage of the Ev.-Lutheran population over 13 years old	5·9%

About one third of the church-goers are men and two thirds women. The age distribution shows the following structure: one third are old people who will soon retire or who are already pensioners; one third are middle-aged married couples, housewives, single middle-aged people, young people; and one third are confirmands who are obliged to attend services during the period of instruction.

Apart from the service on Sunday morning, a regular end-of-week service is held on Saturday evenings, and an occasional evening service is held on Church festivals which are not public holidays. These services bring together only a small number of parishioners, since church-going is customarily connected with Sunday.

PARISH AREA

Average no. in congregation at the Saturday evening service	29
Average attendance at a weekday evening service	62
(Data B)	

The attendance on religious festivals such as Easter, Whitsun, Christmas and Remembrance Sunday does not differ substantially from the normal Sunday attendance. Only the Christmas Eve Vespers and the Confirmation Services, when the year's candidates are confirmed, are exceptions.

PARISH AREA

Average attendance at the four Christmas Eve Vespers	1,452
Percentage of Ev.-Lutheran population attending Christmas Eve Vespers	11·2%
(Data B)	

The children's service is on Sunday morning after the main service. The attendance depends upon the ability of the lay helpers, each of whom instructs a small group before the short service.

	PARISH AREA
Average attendance at Children's Service	61
Average number of helpers at Children's Service	7
(Data B)	

Both at the beginning of the school term and on Reformation Day, services are arranged in collaboration with the State primary schools in the area. The schools and the teachers invite their pupils to attend church and there is almost a 100% response. The church is always full at these times.

The Lord's Supper is as a rule celebrated at the morning service on the first Sunday of the month and at Church festivals. Before the beginning of the Communion service, two thirds of the congregation leave the church—among them, of course, the confirmands, who are not yet allowed to go to the Lord's Supper. This situation is connected with the fact that until recent times the Lord's Supper was regarded in many congregations as a special celebration held after the normal service, and people went usually once or twice a year to Communion.

	PARISH AREA
No. of people receiving communion during the Sunday service in one year	1,628
No. of services including the Lord's Supper in one year	24
Average no. of communicants at each service	68
(Data B)	
Average no. of congregation at one service	213
(Data A)	

To sum up, it must be said that the Christianity of the people in the area of the parish has comparatively little to do with the church services or the Lord's Supper, but on the contrary consists principally in laying claim to the performance of the occasional offices. On the one hand, therefore, there is the 'general Christianity' of the area, and on the other, a piety which is turned towards church services and the congregation.

	CITY OF HAMBURG
Relation of baptisms to births in purely Ev.-Lutheran marriages	87·5%
Funeral services in relation to Ev.-Lutheran deaths	81·7%

CITY OF HAMBURG

Church weddings of purely Ev.-Lutheran couples as percentage of civil ceremonies of purely Ev.-Lutheran couples	55·4%

PARISH AREA

Percentage of Ev.-Lutheran population at Christmas Eve Vespers	11·2%
Percentage of adult Ev.-Lutheran population attending services with any regularity	5·9%
Percentage of Ev.-Lutheran population attending services every Sunday	1·6%
Percentage of Ev.-Lutheran population receiving communion at a service including the Lord's Supper	0·5%

(d) *Parochial activities*

Public activities for the whole congregation are restricted to a fairly small number of occasions. Most popular are the church concerts; next come evening lectures, and then a series of Lenten meditations. Finally, the annual parish bazaar must be mentioned. Publicity for the church concerts is by leaflets and posters. About 100 people usually attend. The lecture series and the Lenten meditation, if only publicized in the monthly parish letter, are attended by about 60 people—barely a third of the Sunday congregation. It is not possible to assess attendance at the parish bazaar, which is a time for general fellowship and raising funds for the charitable activities of the congregation. Its informal atmosphere, allowing one to come and go freely, elicits a good response.

The numbers attending the groups which meet in the evenings (or in the afternoons for children) are below that of normal Sunday church attendance, although the groups have a missionary orientation. Only the children's and youth groups present a more favourable picture. In addition to this, the members of these groups, although largely drawn from worshipping members of the congregation, are by no means all regular church-goers. On the other hand, there is a greater tendency to attend church regularly over the years than to maintain regular membership in a group, so that in the course of time more people pass through a group than the numbers at any given moment may indicate. The number of church-goers who have at one time taken part in a congregational group may be larger than the present numbers indicate. The emphasis laid on group work in the parish can be seen from the following review of the weekly meetings.

NO. OF GROUPS	NAME OF GROUP	LEADER	SUBJECT	TOTAL NO. OF PARTICI-PANTS	PARTICI-PANTS PER GROUP
1	Bible Hour	Pastor	Bible Study	28	28
1	Fireside Group	Pastor	Prayers and subjects of general interest	22	22
1	Women's Group	Pastor's Wife	Prayers and social activities	10	10
1	Choir	Choir leader	Choral singing	35	35
2	Parish workers' groups	Pastor	Visiting, preparation of children's services	12	6
3	Old people's groups	Parish woman worker, parish sister		54	18
5	Youth groups	Lay deacon	Young people aged 15–23	79	16
8	Children's groups	Woman worker, lay deacon	Young people aged 3–13	127	16
8	Confirmation groups	Pastor	Instruction	282	35

(Data B)

	PARISH AREA
Members of groups over 15 years of age, excluding confirmands (multiple membership roughly corrected)	169
Group members over 15 as percentage of average Sunday congregation	79·3%
Members up to 13 years of age in the Children's and Young People's Groups (multiple membership roughly corrected)	77
Group members up to 13 years old as percentage of attendance at children's service	126%

(Data B)

The regular weekly meetings of the groups and circles, together with the confirmation instruction classes, take up the largest part of the fixed time-table of the pastor and similarly that of the lay deacon and parish woman worker.

Fixed appointments of the pastor in an average week:	16 hours
Conducting services	26%
Group work	32%
Confirmation classes	42%
(Data B)	

Even if the conduct of services requires longer preparation than group work, it can be clearly seen how great are the demands made on the pastor by the adults who come to the regular weekly activities and by the young people in the confirmation classes. A pastor who wishes to develop missionary work beyond the round of his weekly engagements must necessarily restrict the time he gives to group activities and instruction. The lay deacon and the woman parish worker lead the numerous groups for children and young people. These groups occupy the lay deacon on three weekday afternoons and evenings and one other weekday afternoon. The woman parish worker is occupied every afternoon and one morning each week with children's groups. Although both the lay deacon and the woman worker have other responsibilities in the congregation, a considerable amount of their energy, like the pastor's, is expended in fulfilling their responsibilities to these groups.

(e) *Welfare work*

The parish maintains a kindergarten and a day nursery. The kindergarten has two groups of 35 upper middle-class children, each looked after by a kindergarten teacher. The pastors are responsible for the running of the kindergarten. The pastors take turns at the beginning of each week in telling the children a Bible story or holding a short service for them in church. Twice a year the parents of the children are invited to a parents' evening.

The day nursery was in fact founded by the Church but the running of it is supported by the State. It takes 50 children of working mothers for the whole day and 15 children for half the day. The staff consists of a woman leader, two kindergarten teachers and two cooks. Here too the pastor leads a short period of worship once a week for the children. The children belong to the lower social groups of the parish.

The parish sister visits and gives help and support to the old and sick people in the parish.

The parish woman worker and the lay deacon are trained in social care. As occasion arises, they concern themselves with cases of need which come to their notice, and work hand in hand with the State social services. They are also responsible for the house to house collectors for church welfare work.

(f) *The financial resources of the parish*

The parish is supported largely from the Church tax. The State col-
lects the Church tax along with income tax (cf. for Church tax, P. Zieger,
'*Die Kirchensteuer in Deutschland*', Luth. Monatshefte, no. 2, 1965, p. 59 f.).
In the Hamburg Regional Church it is 8% of the income tax. From the
large number of wage earners—estimated at about 20–30%—who pay
no tax because their income is below a certain level, a minimum contribution of DM 6 is collected. The Church reimburses the tax offices
for the administrative costs of collecting the Church taxes.

The average annual contribution by each Church member in the
Hamburg Regional Church in 1963 was DM 62·50. In the same year
the income through donations and collections in the parish under
investigation was DM 19,524. The collections and donations support
the welfare work of the congregation, ecumenical activities and matters
which concern the work of the whole Church in Germany. In addition
the charitable and missionary institutions of the Church also receive
direct donations from the public, which do not go through the local
congregation and are not recorded there.

CHAPTER 2

Traditional Concepts and Present Tasks

I. WHAT CONSTITUTES A CHRISTIAN LIFE?

In connection with a forthcoming baptism, I visited the family of a fore-man. The father was a taciturn and straightforward man, and the mother had a simple and happy nature. Both were already middle-aged, and their eldest child, a daughter, was soon to begin confirmation instruction. After a long interval they had had a son, whom I was to baptize. At the beginning of the conversation, I asked if they agreed to a Japanese pastor baptizing their child. The father replied, 'It is all the same to us. You are a pastor. The essential thing is for our little one to be properly baptized.' After I had pointed out the pattern of the baptism service and its significance, I asked if they had any questions. They both said nothing, then the father replied briefly in the negative.

Then we got into conversation. The husband remained reserved, and his wife began to talk. Of course her husband never went to church, and she had never seen him pray or read his Bible. But he was a good Christian because he believed in God, did his work conscientiously and cared for his family. She used to go to church but did so no longer. In her last parish she had had a disagreement with the parish sister. Their 13-year-old daughter, who was shortly to begin her confirmation classes, said grace before meals. The wife admitted to being more of a believer than her husband. She often read her Bible and prayed to God for peace in the family and for her marriage.

The general view of the Christian life is that it is a life which is 'regular'.* This expression 'regular', which is used a great deal today as a standard of value, contains various meanings.

The meaning which a pastor gives to a regular Christian life can be described as follows: a Christian life is that led by those who attend church services and parish activities almost without fail and therefore know the pastor personally. The person who has a private religion but rarely comes to church—there are not in fact many who live by such a personal kind of piety—is in the eyes of the pastor not leading a 'regular' Christian life. This image of Christianity is also shared by the inner circle of the congregation, who regularly support the various parish organizations.

A church member who supposedly belongs to the Church but never attends a service has a different understanding of being a regular Christian. He becomes aware of his understanding of it when he is talking with a foreigner who comes from a different cultural back-ground, or else to someone who does not belong to his own orderly, middle-class world. The kind of understanding of Christianity which he

* *in Ordnung* = in order, all right, regular, &c.

17

then assumes has much in common with a feeling for culture or justice. His knowledge of the Christian faith is actually very slight, but he is familiar with those general customs which are based on the Christian tradition, and in such a conversation is made conscious of them again. A good Christian is one who has no difficulties in his relationships at work or with his friends, acquaintances or family, is a burden to none, and gets on with everyone. The Christian life is completely identified with the life of a normal, decent citizen.

This equation of Christianity with the regular conduct of one's life is understandable in the case of those who are out of touch with the congregation. This view is surprising, however, when one finds it held by members of the congregation who avowedly wish to conform to Christian standards of conduct. The emphasis on order as the chief characteristic of the Christian way of life comes dangerously near to a self-righteous and self-satisfied attitude in the faith. What is the origin of this way of thinking in categories of 'order'?

First, the congregation has a rigidly fixed pattern of organization, and, in order to gather its members together, it is continually necessary to draw attention to and accentuate this pattern. Hence it is easy to define Christian behaviour as conformity to the comprehensive plan of congregational activities. When a person gives positive support to the church's pattern of organization and its goals, then his Christian conviction is objectively present and visible to all. For some time now, the Christian life has been regarded as one which is arranged to fit into the pattern of congregational activities.

In addition to this, church-goers as well as non-church-goers automatically assume that being a Christian consists in the acceptance of generally accepted and established norms of conduct, which have been handed down as customs from previous generations. Whether one adheres to them or takes them seriously is another matter. There is no question of despising the customs and traditions handed down. Most people, however, overlook the fact that these customs and traditions must be tested and checked by them if they are to remain living norms. A critical consideration destroys the automatic acceptance of matters of conduct, and because of this neither church-goers nor non-church-goers are very anxious to undertake it.

Finally, Christians in Europe can regard the question of Christian conduct as a simple matter, because they approach other religions with such a naïve air of superiority. But they are so self-confident in their attitude to other beliefs merely because their own is rooted in highly civilized and technically developed countries. Christianity benefits from comparison between the different standards of civilization and technical development which exist in the world. The fact that standards of conduct which are called Christian in the western world would in the East be called Mohammedan or Buddhist, should provide the congregation with food for thought. Many forms of religious conduct are, externally speaking, absolutely identical. The world's religions no longer differ very much in the characteristics of their religious-institutional life. All include prayer, scripture readings, doctrinal instruction, attendance at centres of worship, works of charity and missionary activity.

Although the Christian life is often thought of in terms of order, whether in congregational arrangements or in social customs, it is a fact that the attitude of a Christian can never be said to be perfected or 'in order'. As a Christian, he is always in a state of becoming or growing, regardless of whether he attends church services regularly or only rarely gives any thought to what constitutes being a Christian. The Christian life, therefore, cannot be said to be based on principles laid down once for all, or on ways of life deduced from them which are regarded as universally valid. The Christian life grows out of belief and reveals itself in a spontaneous reaction to people and social situations. Here there is as much need for conscience as for common sense, a need for a sense of timeliness as well as a rational grasp and understanding. This flexibility is the exact opposite of a 'regular Christian way of living'. It is characterized by the paradoxical fact that man is at the same time a sinner and one who is justified before God. If a person thinks that his life is in the Christian sense 'in order', then he again finds himself drawn into a movement of 'becoming' and is shown afresh the direction which leads to being a Christian. The claim that one's conduct is definitively 'in order' is the opposite of real Christianity.

Endeavouring to bring a certain order into one's own conduct, one's family life and one's relations with others, is in fact one of the strongest natural impulses. But this natural impulse contains at the same time the danger of self-righteousness. Self-righteousness is always connected with a certain narrow-mindedness and a feeling of being on the defensive. Both these characteristics can easily lead to a lack of healthy respect for human nature and a lack of mutual trust in one's fellow-men. Instead of thinking and discussing together to find new ways, there is only the right or the wrong solution. Instead of being a help, these principles of order serve only to support a legalism, which may indeed encourage certain standards of conduct, but fails to meet people in their actual situations. It is customary to say in the congregation that it is very important at the present time to emphasize the obligatory nature of the contents of the Ten Commandments. It is probably true to say that, with the break-up of the traditional Christian life based on custom, the Ten Commandments have also come to be regarded as less binding. But the main concern of the congregation should not lie here.

The likelihood that Christian conduct will be visible in society in the future is also much more closely related to the extent to which it shows flexibility and lack of prejudice. The conditions of modern society only serve to increase respect for legalism. Today everything is judged by expediency and tested for its appropriateness. In public and private life one will no longer be able to manage without the rule of law and order. The individual's sense of order is being continually strengthened by organization and planning. In this situation, the decisive role of

Christian belief can be said to lie precisely in overcoming ways of thinking which are phrased only in terms of order. Christian conduct will reveal itself where the individual in his way of life protests against society's riding roughshod, in the name of order, over the freedom and dignity of man. Christian conduct will not truly be seen in preoccupation with over-organized forms of Church life; it will be concerned with human existence before God.

2. THE FUNCTION OF THE CHURCH SERVICE

One of my colleagues in the parish buried an elderly lady from his part of the parish; at the funeral service he preached to the best of his ability about the message of death and resurrection. The mourners, however, found his address lacking in concern because he had not expressly praised the departed and had only spoken about Christian truths. The relatives were angry about this. Soon afterwards the husband of the deceased also died. The relatives then turned to another pastor, to whose area they did not belong, with a request to perform the burial. He, however, put them in touch again with the pastor who was responsible. After some thought my colleague undertook this second burial. The same people were present at the funeral as before. This time, however, they were all very pleased with what the pastor said because in his short address he had praised the departed in accordance with his merits.

After the services on Christmas Eve, the verger told me that on the way out some of those who attended church expressed their annoyance by saying, 'Why must the pastor preach even on Christmas Eve?'

On major festivals and at the occasional offices, two quite different concerns tend to overlap. The pastor is anxious to use the opportunity to reach with the gospel message those to whom he normally never preaches. The congregation, on the other hand, is expecting quiet recollection in a solemn atmosphere. Even at the ordinary Sunday services, this kind of difference between the expectations on either side can arise, and the church council spends a long time considering such matters as whether the collection should be taken on the way out instead of in the middle of the service. The movement of those taking the collection in the middle of the service, they feel, tends to disturb its solemnity.

For a congregation, the church service performs three functions:

First, it presents an opportunity to satisfy the need for solemnity. What an individual means by solemnity varies with his aesthetic judgment and the habits he has acquired since childhood. Every local or regional church has its traditional form of service and particular ceremonial solemnity. The arrangement of the building, the orderly course of the service, the attitude of those present, the playing of the organ, the singing, the pastor's voice and its tone, all these contribute to a serious atmosphere and a reflective attitude, and meet that need for composure and solemnity which is present in every man. The church service does everything possible to satisfy the aesthetic tastes of all those present.

Secondly, the church service facilitates participation in an activity of public significance. This function of the service is of decisive importance for those people who in other spheres of life are not yet, or are no longer, regarded as equal partners in public discussion or public activities. For them, the service is an important gathering at which they are more welcome than elsewhere, and find friendly acceptance. Old people and those who feel that socially they have been pushed into the background often look at the service from this point of view, though without fully realizing it themselves. Whereas in public affairs they are often passed over quickly and easily, in the congregation a place is kept open for them where they can represent matters of important general concern. The same is true of young people who take part in the adult services when they are being prepared for confirmation (from the age of 13 to 14). In the eyes of adults, they are still too young for many things, yet at the service they are taken as equals into an affair which is of importance and solemn significance for adults. At many Sunday services the nave of the church is filled with confirmands and elderly people.

In the third place, the service is the place where the Word of God is proclaimed in the sermon and in the sacrament of the Lord's Supper. This is the essential function of the service. Almost all people who come to a service chiefly expect something from the sermon. Many church members do not mind which pastor preaches. Others will attend only the service at which a particular pastor is scheduled to preach. In a town it is possible to choose which Sunday service one will attend according to who is preaching. The service and sermon are something taken for granted. Only a few people go to church because of a personal urge to seek for clarity and consolation through the Gospel. In such a case the motives are doubt, the problem of coping with life, or even, on occasions, the shock of an event—for example, the murder of President Kennedy. When the service includes a celebration of the Lord's Supper, in the congregation under survey about a third of those present receive the sacrament. It is difficult to say what the individual takes home from his encounter with the Word of God in sermon and sacrament. But in any case the service provides a regular place for this encounter.

At all services great care is taken to ensure that these three elements of solemnity, public character and proclamation are fully and completely realized. The price to be paid for this, however, is that the pastor and his full-time assistants must play a uniquely decisive role in the service. They are the only ones who are able to perform these functions in the service, in that traditional way which isolates them from associations with normal social life. This produces a remarkable effect. The congregation is divided into speakers and listeners, actors and spectators. The service can take on the character of a public performance of sacrosanct cultural ritual, and the members of the congregation in the body of the church can receive the impression that they are doing nothing more than supporting and promoting this performance by their presence. There is a danger that the members of the congregation may, on the one hand, feel themselves, as defenders of Christendom, to be superior to those outside and yet, at the same time, to suffer from an inferiority complex because what takes place inside the church has long since lost its interest for contemporary society. The sermon often serves to encourage the hearers in an outward feeling of superiority, but nevertheless, by its arguments, to strengthen the minority feeling even further.

Behind all this lies the decisive separation between church-goers and non-church-goers. For the church-goers the service is 'their affair'. The non-church-goers assume that they have nothing to do with what normally takes place in the service, and it would never occur to them that they were missing anything by staying away from it. For them being a Christian does not reside in church attendance, but in the living of a decent, irreproachable life. They know little of the significance of the church service and the congregation. The church-goers concern themselves equally little about the origins of the misunderstandings and prejudices of the others, and regard the indifference of the non-church-goers as a simple fact, even though they are meeting them all the time in the circle of their friends and colleagues. This stereotyped division of people into church-goers and non-church-goers reveals widespread indifference towards whether or not a person ought to play any part in the life of the Church.

But even those who do attend church do not regard the service as a community action which strengthens the corporate sense. Church-going is for them a private act, the roots of which lie more in their personal Christian profession than in the building up of a group. The pastor and the full-time assistants are responsible for seeing that the singing, praying and confession of the faith are a common action, and that a sense of community is thereby established during the service. It seems strange that the pastor should address this gathering of many individuals as 'Liebe Gemeinde' or 'Dear Congregation', and that the notices and intercessions automatically presuppose common interests. The pastor ought in fact to express the particular intercessions and notices in such a way that each member of the congregation can make them fully his own. When the political community and the religious community were identical, there may have been some point in emphasizing the generally accepted common concerns. Today, when most people attend the service as individuals and feel very little in common with the other participants, emphasis on a generally accepted common concern can seem artificial (cf. the data on the mobility of the population, p. 7.)

It is neither possible to build the church services around a small group of individuals who assemble like a conventicle for an intimate fellowship, nor can one arrange the services so that all the members of the local congregation and inhabitants of the parish can take part in them. It is important to gain acceptance for the point of view that the service is not an occasion for the Church to display itself. Its purpose does not lie in exhibiting the support which the Church has from society, thereby lending weight to its claims on society. The service is the point of departure of the action and gift of God, which extend beyond the institutional Church and its concerns, and beyond the quiet hour of Sunday morning contemplation. The service is important because God deals with men in Word and Sacrament. In the face of this, the point of view that the congregation must keep together takes on a secondary importance. When an individual church-goer understands the service as God's dealing with him, he can no longer just think of the church service in relation to himself alone; he comes to appreciate how his neighbour in the pew also lives under the same action of God as himself. This action of God is not confined to the service, but is as much concerned with those who never attend church as with the church-goers.

It is inappropriate, therefore, to regard church services, and in particular the occasional offices, as an opportunity to convert people from the world to the congregation. It is much more important to assist them to acquire a deeper conviction and a less limited understanding of their tasks as Christians. Church-goers have continually to learn afresh what the service gives to them, and in what direction it leads them to act. Whether one regards all that happens in the service as an act of self-preservation or as one of following Christ is of decisive importance.

3. ARE CHURCH GROUPS NECESSARY?

An invitation was extended to a meeting in the church hall, with the title 'Parish Meeting', at which it was proposed to introduce the candidates for election to the Church Council. The number present, including the candidates and the parish staff, was 120. Only a small percentage of the Protestants living in the parish area was interested. The pastor, who chaired the meeting, in his opening remarks expressed regret at the state of affairs revealed by the poor attendance. The astonishing thing about the 'Parish Meeting' was not so much the small number of people present, in contrast to the number of nominal church members, as the fact that those present were all members of the groups which meet during the week.

When one is concerned with the question of how the congregation can grow or extend its work, the first and almost the only idea which comes up is that of forming small groups to meet on evenings during the week. They offer an opportunity for personal conversation and discussion. The pastor announces the meetings of these groups at the Sunday service, and the congregation is continually being invited to join these groups. To attract people to the groups and give them some indication of the make-up of the gatherings, they are arranged according to age and sex. Alternatively, the circles make their appeal through the particular subjects which are discussed in them. One example is the Bible study group found in most parishes. The number of such fellowships and the support they receive show whether congregational life is flourishing or not. Every attempt to stimulate activity in the parish with some missionary effect is concentrated on spending time and energy in strengthening these small parish groups. It is a natural thing that small groups should be formed for discussion and fellowship. They arise everywhere where people are linked together in a common concern. It is, however, quite another thing for the entire initiative of a congregation, and in particular its full-time staff, to be applied to the maintenance and organization of such groups. The natural existence of subsidiary groups and small fellowships is nevertheless often elevated into a programme which is presented as the sole task of the congregation, and absorbs the entire working time of the full-time staff and the pastor.

The more the congregation as an institution, and the leaders of the groups, appeal for participation, the more detached the individual tends to be in relation to this type of fellowship. The participants ask themselves what use such opportunities for meeting in the congregation are to them. The possibility of finding good fellowship or of conversing about particular subjects can make regular attendance worth while. However, they are welcomed to each evening as invited guests, not as those who are running their own concern. They can at any time put in an appearance or stay away without their absence having any consequences. This is because the initiative does not lie in the group itself but entirely on the side of the host.

In fact congregational groups tend to turn in upon themselves. The groups are mostly not well known to the public, and people who have no firm attachment to the Church do not know what, apart from the church services, actually takes place on the church premises. If events do take place under church auspices, outsiders tend to treat them sceptically, since their understanding of Christianity excludes the institutional role of the Church. Because people are not aware of the aim of the congregation's activities, and cannot label these meetings satisfactorily, it is customary to speak slightingly of what they have to offer. The groups are anxious, in accordance with their aims, to remain open at all costs. Everyone is to be welcome. But the honest endeavour to practise openness comes up against strong resistance in the social environment, where people do not wish to be concerned with purely churchly activities. Despite their aim to be open, their isolation from the outside world turns the groups very much in upon themselves. As a result, they quickly develop a certain homogeneity and increasingly seek their support within the congregation. Thus it occurs that those groups which are supposed to be working against the narrowing of the congregation in fact serve to strengthen the congregation's separation from society. The strong forces here at work are very hard to break down, because the groups are no longer able to approach outsiders but try to claim each new participant for themselves.

The homogeneity and churchliness of these groups creates a strong sense of fellowship internally. In the case of youth groups, the fellowship usually does not last so long, because young people are not yet finally settled in their way of life and their interests. Young people still face changes in their circumstances which could lead them in com-

pletely different directions. Most of the adult groups concern themselves
with particular subjects, so that the central features should really be
discussion and interest in spiritual matters. But even here, fellowship
becomes in time the strongest feature, on account of the regularity of
the meetings and of the unanimous opinions which the subject matter
engenders. The result for many members is that their lives as Christians
come to be identified with the social relationships involved in their
membership of the group.

The cleavage between the activities on church premises and the
fellowship peculiar to the congregation on the one hand, and normal
social contacts on the other, could most easily be overcome in two ways.

First, single themes should be selected which are of topical and
general interest and, perhaps, practical as well. They can be
thoroughly Christian without their treatment necessarily being narrowly
ecclesiastical or theological. The evenings should not take place regularly but occasionally, and with varying subjects. Each individual
evening requires preparation and a special invitation.

Secondly, those who come to the meeting should be able to speak and
take part. From the beginning, it must be the intention that those
present are to be brought out of the role of mere hearers and spectators,
and led into that of participation. The organizer must be careful to
avoid behaving like a teacher, but must, with all others, learn from the
general discussion.

If this type of activity is to be brought a stage nearer its real goal, it is
necessary to alter the character of the composition of the groups. There
is one preliminary change to be made. Today each group is as a rule
still under the direction of one of the parish staff, usually the pastors.
It is they who actually hold the groups together. The character of the
meetings depends on their personality, and the existence of a church
group is unthinkable without them. The inherited principle of a community formed around a person in authority still determines the nature
of these groups, although, superficially, they run themselves 'demo-
cratically'. The primary need for a group is a full-time leader who
preserves its communal character. Horizontal relationships between
the members of the group come second.

In groups constructed in such a way, everything naturally depends
on the personality of the leader and his ability to lead. Because of this,
attendance at their circles is, for the members of the staff, a direct
indication of their achievements in the congregation. They cultivate
their groups as if they were their private property and thereby, without
realizing it, continually limit the autonomy of the participants. Many of
the members may have managed to exercise patience in the matter of
the leader's personality, but an outsider who is not acquainted with
church groups would at once feel himself patronized and restricted in
his personal freedom.

If group members were responsible for their own circle and each
group were really autonomous, the staff could save much time and
energy which they could invest in the spiritual and organizational

preparation of the work in the parish. When the members of the groups are themselves responsible and have to develop the work, they will much sooner recognize where they need help and encouragement, where their weaknesses lie and what basic knowledge they lack. Each will then realize that his group is neither a 'preparation class' for loyal church attendance nor simply a lecture forum, but a way of equipping the Christian with the means to make his own decisions. The hazy motivation of the groups in the congregation, their introvertedness and the limited independence of the participants are inherited from the church life of yesterday. Perhaps tomorrow's congregation will be organized in quite a different way, but it is possible to envisage the future tasks of the Church only by looking at the narrow community which today lives on group work.

4. THE ROLE OF THE PASTOR

As I approached the parsonage on my way home one day, a young post office worker caught up with me. He had obviously finished his day's work and was in a very good mood. He engaged me in conversation with considerable familiarity. As we reached the place where I lived, and I walked more slowly, he asked me, 'Where do you live, then?' I told him and pointed to the house. When he saw that it was the parsonage and he realized that he had a pastor in front of him, his expression changed. He said not another word and went quickly on his way, so that we did not even have time to say good-bye to one another. It would have been fine if the parsonage had had no such associations for him!

The pastor is rated as a professional man. Preparation for the ministry is long, necessitating a certain degree of financial support from the family, and the pastor is classed as an academic. The tasks of the pastoral office are generally believed to include the following responsibilities.

The pastor has first to maintain the church organization in his area. In a large town he often has the support of two or three colleagues. He is responsible for the church buildings and the congregational activities which take place in the church hall, such as the kindergarten and group work. Under him are those persons who are employed by the church and share his work in the congregation, such as the deacon and the organist. The pastor draws up general plans for the work of the parish and is responsible for their execution. He is responsible too for publicity in the area, and for the ways in which people are invited into the congregation. Both the central church authorities and society as a whole accept without question the pastor's role as an organizer and administrator.

Secondly, the pastor has the task of representing the Church as a sacral institution. In the occasional offices, religious instruction, preaching and the administration of the sacraments, the pastor has a decisive authority that derives from his office. He alone can carry out these functions appropriately and validly proclaim the content of the

Christian faith. Despite all the personal limitations which a pastor may have, he is bound to the Church by the office which has been committed to him once and for all, in the sense that wherever he may be present he makes visible the Church and the tradition of the Christian faith. A large part of his theological training is designed with this representational activity in mind, and his spiritual initiative in his work is moulded by it.

Alongside his tasks as organizer and representative stands a third, personal, characteristic which is included in the general view of his occupation. It is not sufficient for the pastor to be a good organizer and give an objective presentation of the faith; he must also personally live and act by his beliefs. A man cannot be committed to an inner attitude of this kind either by the authorities of the Church or his spiritual office. It is only by faithfulness to his vocation from God that he can come to recognize his calling in this personal way and in this depth. In contrast to all external pressures, only the pastor's personal desire to carry out his commission conscientiously before God is of any effect here. People often express this personal side of a pastor's life as being important to them by saying that their pastor does not have to be a 'great preacher' or an intellectually-gifted man, but that, as a person, he should radiate a spiritual power that interprets Christian existence and the proclamation of the Word in a way to compel belief.

It is a fact that the pastor expends his major energies on the first two tasks, i.e. in the preparation and conduct of church services and activities, and in administration. Day after day he puts all his energies into the maintenance of an organization which in the modern world seems outdated, somewhat like a brave sea captain fighting to right his sinking ship, or like a person who has inherited an old-established business, handed down from generation to generation, and who endeavours to keep it going despite the fact that no one today has any interest in it. The dignity of his office, rooted in a centuries-old tradition, makes him assume heavy obligations in his work as a representative of the faith and of the Christian ministry. In this, the following are the most important problems with which he is daily faced.

Above all, the pastor feels very strongly that his sphere of influence is necessarily restricted to a particular circle of people. He may indeed, as a pastor, know many people who have had occasional dealings with him on a personal or official basis, but he has continuous contact only with those who attend church services regularly, who are present at congregational activities or are among his circle of personal friends.

Furthermore, the pastor finds himself continuously concerned with a large number of matters which must be finished by a given time, with the result that the numerous tasks he has to carry out put him under continuous pressure of time. This pressure means that the pastor rarely has leisure to reflect on the problems on hand, or to spend much time with his family. Because it is so difficult for him to see his work objectively, his practical ideas and spiritual thoughts easily turn into fixed views and simple formulas.

Without wishing to do so, he can very quickly lose sight of those people who need his help as a pastor but do not belong to his congregation or his circle of friends. A person who is in despair or needs advice does not come at the official times for interviews, and yet he wants someone to talk to and to advise him. Others are very seriously concerned with questions of truth and they would like to meet someone who understands these matters. It would mean too much fuss to make a point of calling on the pastor. People suppose that he has not got time for a personal conversation. His official duties, as the pastor is well aware, do not leave him time to meet these people and to talk with them.

If the pastor does in fact succeed in overcoming the difficulties and problems inherent in his work, it is because he is conscious that, as a pastor, he has a special vocation. This knowledge liberates a great deal of energy and enables him to be very persevering in his work.

Thus, as he goes about his daily work, the pastor can be conscious of the fact of belonging to the clergy. He is a respected person, and his work is reckoned as belonging to those old and recognized callings which are important for the order of society and social values. Because of his training the pastor is an 'academic'. It is generally believed that for an academic career he needs above-average intelligence. Therefore social esteem and his level of education serve to lift the pastor above the level of other occupations. The pastor can see himself belonging to a particular order in society which, in a special way, bears responsibility and must be active in leadership. At a time when many people are indifferent to the congregation and the Church, or believe that they can simply break with traditional values, the pastor is helped by the consciousness of representing a profession with a claim to spiritual leadership. This support enables him to carry on his work with conviction, and gives him the advantage of being able, instead of breaking with tradition, to separate the essential from the outdated and to renew the heritage of the past to fit the needs of the present. On the other hand, the consciousness that he is a member of a spiritual *élite* lends his ministry a characteristic air of self-sufficiency. Those who from a distance take an interest in the work of the Church and the Christian faith are put off by finding in the clergy a certain self-satisfaction which is impervious to any criticism from the general public.

In addition, recent years have seen the growth amongst pastors of a tendency to regard the ministry as one profession amongst many others which has its special problems. Industrial and bureaucratic society exists on the principle of a division of labour, and each occupation has its clearly defined sphere of activity which makes particular demands on a person. The pastor stands up for his calling, but he does not insist upon the idea that his work is more honourable or more important than any other. It is simply that his occupation has a sphere of activity which belongs to it alone. Because he has once chosen this calling, he must now in his ministry fit himself to meet the relevant demands which face him as a pastor. Because he feels that, spiritually speaking, he owes something to many people, he adheres above all to the tasks which can formally and appropriately be required of him in accordance with his office. In face of many possibilities of seizing the initiative, he concentrates his activity instead on those duties for which, as an office-bearer and representative of the Church, he can be held responsible. While he is technically responsible for the administration of the Church, in corresponding fashion the church authorities are the body to which he must turn if he wishes anything done. The central church bodies are responsible for all improvements concerning his conditions of work and personal circumstances. This technical understanding of their work is found increasingly amongst the younger pastors, and forms an astonishing contrast to the situation of the pastors in non-Western churches, who from the outset are obliged to practise elasticity and improvisation in their ministry.

Thirdly, in his work the pastor carries the knowledge of his spiritual commission to proclaim the Gospel. This spiritual commission is not an isolated reality, but is the basis of the dignity of the pastoral office and provides an outline of the sphere of technical activity towards which the pastor's particular vocation is aimed.

Nevertheless, the connection between the pastor's awareness of his position and his spiritual commission is today becoming more and more ambiguous. If the pastor belongs to the particular rank of 'clergy', then he is not an ordinary man following his particular profession, but is surrounded by a certain holiness which marks his whole life. His exalted position supports the conviction that he embodies the faith and the Church in all that he does. In urban conditions such an inherited image of the pastor plays a decreasing part, and the opposite idea is gaining acceptance. It is not the pastor's status which conveys, through his pattern of life, what the content of the pastoral office is. People rather examine each pastor to see how far he acts in accordance with a spiritual conviction and decision, although he is a pastor and belongs to the ranks of the clergy. The pastor's bearing of inner conviction wins recognition and respect, while the mere consciousness of status meets with disapproval.

Consciousness of the spiritual commission is more closely connected with the concept of the pastoral office as one profession among others. The special requirements of this profession consist in proclaiming the word through worship, giving religious instruction, and administering the sacraments. Preaching, teaching and administration of the sacraments, which constitute the pastor's office, guarantee that his spiritual commission is respected. But it is questionable whether this commission to proclaim the Gospel can be conceived simply and solely in terms of fixed professional duties. To fulfil the commission completely, it is not sufficient only to think of what happens in church buildings and during the liturgy and worship of the church.

The person who feels called to the office of a preacher of the gospel enters upon an ecclesiastical office with attendant obligations. There is not a single pastor who does not wish to fulfil these obligations conscientiously. However, the mere performance of such institutional duties is inadequate for the fulfilment of the wider vocation to the spiritual commission to proclaim the gospel. There is no pastor who would not like to be a shepherd and an ideal pastor, in the sense that he had the time and strength for personal conversations with those who are seekers, both within and without the congregation. If a pastor continually finds that he is being compelled to neglect his pastoral commission, the ultimate decision lies in his hands through the priorities which he sets in his work. Although the congregation with its structure binds him, and the prescribed course of parish life cuts into his free time, he is still free to choose whether to regard his work more in terms of his status-consciousness and professional duties or in terms of a calling from God. If he is reasonably competent and handles the organizational tasks intelligently, it is possible for him to do justice to his professional duties and at the same time remain true to his spiritual calling. Naturally the professional aspects are always pressing for recognition. But professional concerns do not build bridges between people; this is done only through that spiritual commission which the pastor has to fulfil with his whole personality.

5. RESPONSIBILITY OF THE LAITY

A girl student in the congregation gave German lessons to a Japanese girl, and a friendship developed between the two. When the Japanese girl, after much doubting, finally considered accepting the Christian faith, it was, above all, this student who gave her the courage to make her decision. Before the Japanese girl said what was in her mind, this student had neither invited her friend to come to church nor spoken about the Christian faith. When, one day, the Japanese girl of her own accord asked about it, she spoke openly about her convictions and said what belief meant to her. Her attitude and her faith were of such help to the Japanese girl that she shortly afterwards decided to ask for baptism. The German student is very retiring by nature; she goes to church almost every Sunday, without being much noticed. She does not belong to a parish group, but is occasionally seen at a lecture meeting. She was present at the Japanese girl's baptism and was the only German who took part in the service.

In the traditional parish system, lay co-operation and responsibility are restricted simply to participation in parish activities. Presence at meetings is regarded as the same as interest in the congregation's concerns, so that a church member can regulate his relationship to the Church by attendance at its activities. There are various behaviour patterns in the frequency of attendance. Participation has simply to be arranged in one pattern or another. The layman's responsibility, then, is seen to consist in his adherence in some degree to a Christian habit, for example Sunday church-going, or at any rate in his support of the common activities of the congregation. Members of the congregation make no use at all of their own rights in the matter of co-operation and planning. Generally speaking, the Protestant's detached attitude to his Church and the Roman Catholic layman's lack of independence are partly responsible for this.

Widespread passivity has its roots as much in the historical situation as in the socio-psychological situation of modern man. Today a person is primarily concerned with preserving his private life and keeping it in balance. If one emerges from one's anonymity and undertakes any kind of public task, one's private life is radically disturbed. A person's private life and his circle of acquaintances present numerous, very concrete and incisive obligations. Here people have very definite expectations, and one has indispensable obligations to one's family and relatives. Hence the members of the congregation consider that the public activities of the congregation should be represented by the clergy, who are professionally involved in this sphere. Responsibility for what goes on in the church lies with the pastor. Church-goers and non-church-goers may differ in the frequency of their participation in congregational life, but both generally agree in not regarding the congregation as the central point of their Christian existence. For this reason, most church activities have the character of a monologue and there is little participation by those present.

The monologue in congregational activities proceeds wholly from a confusion of Christian belief with belonging to a church or a religion. Regular attendance does not in fact lead to a responsible attitude in the congregation; it rather serves to relieve a person of further obligations. Very few people identify themselves with the congregation so deeply as to be able to say, 'I can be a Christian only to the extent to which the congregation that I belong to recognizes and fulfils its commission'. When, however, in the present situation a few people consciously throw themselves in with the congregation and work in it—and every congregation relies on a small circle of active laity of this kind—they tend more to fit into the existing structure of the congregation than to press independently for the fulfilment of their own ideas; they make themselves available to assist the existing leadership in ordering the life of the congregation and thus enable the full-time staff to extend their sphere of influence.

The congregation will be changed from a forum for church activities into a place where a deeper understanding and a new kind of obedience is created only when the laity come to understand the representational service they have to give. The various spheres of life from which they come are represented by them within the congregation, and in their various callings and social circumstances they represent the congregation to which they know they are linked. In the congregation, they see to it that the actual situations of their particular spheres of life are always known, and they reveal the concerns of the men with whom they have contact; in their social environment they are the interpreters of the faith and the congregation. The willingness of so many people to attend the congregation and its activities represents a strong potential force. Usually this potential never achieves engagement with the social environment, but remains relatively ineffectual in its private and personal motivations. Here it is necessary to fill in bit by bit the deep cleft between the Church with its monologue-activities and the world which surrounds it; the bridge must be built both by the congregation and by the individual church member. What takes place in the congregation must be made relevant to and fruitful for the world outside. The social experiences of each member in his or her profession and social life must be brought into the congregation and play their part there. The place of the layman is at the meeting-point of these two movements, and it is there that he has his responsibility. It must be his concern to keep continually alive in the congregation a movement of understanding between the Gospel and those aspects of social existence which extend beyond the boundaries of family and private life. He takes into his social environment what he experiences in the congregation, and he passes on to the congregation the impulses he receives and feels in his daily life.

The individual Christian cannot remain passive in his social life in the face of events, whether they concern a particular colleague or wider problems. Faith provides a Christian with the instrument to determine clearly what he has to do for other people in these particular circumstances. He is not making proper use of the instrument of faith by merely endeavouring to bring other people into church activities and getting them to attend church. Faith it is which inspires the Christian to share the burden of his fellow-men and to understand better what his neighbour needs. If he makes good use of his faith at the right moment, men will soon ask him why he behaves in this way and not in another, and what his guiding principle is. Then the Christian tells of the basis of his conviction, and he can do so in the same language as his questioner. In this way, the layman translates by word and deed the Gospel which is proclaimed in the congregation and through the Church.

On the other hand, as a member of his congregation the layman interprets to the Church the kind of expectations which the men with whom he deals have concerning the Church. In the congregation he draws attention to the trends of opinion 'outside', so that the Church can enter into a living dialogue with events in society. The task of the pastor and his staff consists in transposing the information into practice, and carrying out the suggestions that are generally regarded as necessary. A member of the congregation who is giving personal expression in his daily life to his Christianity is unable just to keep silent and think only of himself. He is continually concerned with the questions and needs of his neighbours; he represents to the Church their questions, doubts and prejudices, and thus makes himself the advocate of his environment, even when those outside the congregation have not asked him to do so.

For this two-fold task of applying his belief in the situations of his own daily life and bringing his own problems and circumstances into the Church's proclamation, a Christian needs a congregation in which he feels at home and in which he as a layman has a secure place. This congregation is then really 'his' congregation, to which he belongs completely. And yet, despite this personal relationship, an individual will not regard the congregation as a closed circle of like-minded persons. He will discover how a congregation is essentially a place where room is made for other attitudes and opinions; out of its strong cohesion it is continually adapting itself to become a community where others too can find a place. The revolution in the Church can be conceived of only as a revolution from below, arising from a new understanding of the task of the laity.

6. CONGREGATIONAL WELFARE WORK IN THE 'AFFLUENT SOCIETY'

An old lady whose family live in Eastern Germany and who has no friends in West Germany received permission to visit her home again. However, while staying with her relations she became seriously ill with jaundice, and with the help of the Red Cross was brought back to the hospital in Hamburg. When she was discharged from hospital, but still had to stay in bed, she had nobody who could help her. The parish woman worker looked after the necessities and asked me to visit the woman. During my first visit the woman did not speak a word, but spent the time crying. Within the course of several months she became quieter and was able to talk to me about her past. Eighteen months later she was well again, and one Sunday I saw her at Communion.

In the transitional phase between traditional and industrial society, the congregation became a centre for its area where fellowship, further education and cultural activities, and in particular social welfare, had their proper place (cf. the history of the congregation, p. 6). The combination of activities which came to be associated with the congregation during this period were then gradually divided up between specialist, private or State institutions. Thus social welfare is an activity which today is being intensively taken over by the State in co-operation with the voluntary associations. At the beginning of the industrial revolution, when many people were in need because of insecure economic conditions and because urbanization uprooted them from their normal social surroundings, the congregations felt obliged to come to the rescue. The founders of church welfare movements and institutions did not do their work with the intention of building up their own organizations, but with the aim of alleviating present need and calling people to sacrificial action on behalf of the socially depressed. The more the State then built up its own welfare work, the more the influence of the individual congregations declined in this type of service activity. In today's society there are also people who suffer from need and require assistance, but they can be adequately helped only on a long-term basis, through measures taken by the State and through the work of voluntary (including church) social institutions organized on a national basis. When an individual congregation carries on social work, it is dependent on the support of the State or central church organization.

It is understandable, therefore, that little evidence of notable initiative or personal willingness to help in the realm of traditional social work can be seen in any parish in a normal area. But the fact that the congregation has lost its previous strong position in charitable works does not dispose of the question of diaconal service. It merely compels the congregation to reject any illusions that it can be effective in society in any way other than through action and proclamation springing from belief. The fact that the Welfare State relieves the congregation of the burden of general social care can help Christians to assume a pioneer role and direct their attention to those needs which a clumsy administrative system and social legislation cannot yet comprehend. The congregation should offer its help in those sectors of life where the Welfare State and the social organizations cannot reach, whether because there is no legal provision for such help or because the need is not generally recognized. A congregation is sufficiently free and mobile to react in such cases. Furthermore, the congregation has no occasion to complain about the loss of its functions, for on the contrary the welfare activity of the State and the voluntary organizations opens for them a broad field for co-operation with other social institutions in the district. The congregation, which is faced as a rule with comparative indifference in its locality, can make use of such co-operation to make clear its participation in the life of the whole local community. Discerning, long-term, voluntary co-operation in the tackling of social problems bears witness to those outside to that love which springs from belief, and at the same time renews the inner vitality of the congregation.

The needs which press on people have changed today. The individual with his personal questions and worries gets small consideration in urban society. Modern man feels that he is left alone to face his personal questions about life and, because he cannot express them or solve them, he becomes increasingly isolated and unsure of himself. Contemporary man is convinced that ultimately no one can help him but himself, and that therefore there is no one who is ready to share his problems and help him bear them. The basic notion that each person must care for his own personal problems leads to a lack of trust in other people, and nervous anxiety and frustration lie beneath the outward calm with which life seems to run its course. People take great pains, with considerable success, to improve their outward standard of living. But deep down they are looking for a place of refuge where they can find peace and permanent security. Isolation, and the discord between the outward demands of the standard of living and a person's inner needs, lay increasingly heavy burdens on many people. If someone had been ready at the right moment to give good advice and support, the crisis could have been avoided or diverted. If someone, through openness and willingness to share a problem, had given the individual courage, he might easily have found his feet again. The pastor, his staff and the members of the congregation will be unable to fulfil this need as long as they are overburdened with parish organizations, thereby being drawn into the same type of anxieties and frustrations as other people.

If one is to have time for individuals in need, and to be able to support them with help and advice, it is necessary to take a hard look at

parish work. In face of the power of tradition and custom, it is continually necessary to examine anew what is important in the parish,
in terms of time and energy expended. Furthermore, with all the goodwill in the world, one can do nothing if one does not know if someone in
the area is in need of advice and support. It is essential to have an
information network created by members of the congregation who
know their neighbours. Finally, service to one's neighbour can never be
carried out in a particularist way. Each congregation should be able to
rely on further help from a neighbouring parish in the town if it has
no one with the necessary abilities itself or if, in a particular case,
another congregation has more competent personnel or special experience. Equally does the individual congregation have need of the
particular expert knowledge and abilities of the church welfare
organizations. It is necessary, if adequate help and advice are to be
provided, to bridge the gulf which often exists between the local church
and the central organizations. But even here the congregation must not
work in a particularist way by linking its help with 'missionary'
intentions. The individual Christian and the congregation, when they
help those in need, act out of confidence in their faith and not in order
to strengthen the congregation. The help they offer would lose the
mark of neighbourly love, were the impression given that it was offered
only in order to bring a person back to the Church or to Christian
belief.

Diaconal service today is unthinkable without spiritual insight into
the tasks befitting the congregation, knowledge of the needs of the people
who live in the district, and co-operation between all those in a position
to help.

7. ADVERTISING AND PARISH PUBLICITY

At a meeting of the Church Council consideration was given to an offer
from the Hamburg Underground Railway to give the congregation preferen-
tial treatment in the matter of renting an advertisement showcase in the new
Underground station near the church. The Church Council did not take up
the offer, because it said the congregation needed no publicity and already
had its own notice board at the church hall, which was considered sufficient
advertisement.

On the first birthday of a child I had baptized, I visited the family. The
wife was very surprised to have a visit from a pastor. The child's grand-
father, who had resigned his membership of the Church long ago and had
very little interest in the Christian faith, joined in our conversation. He said
he did not find it surprising that the pastor visited the child, since he had a
great deal of time to do this. For he only had to work once a week on Sunday
mornings. Fortunately I was able in conversation to correct his view of the
parish situation.

As a means of communication with the public, publicity is for the
congregation just as important as the type of communication which
arises in the Sunday services. However, there is a prejudice in the congregation against publicity. This is because people associate it with the

commercial advertising with which they are familiar, and they are anxious to keep the Church free from commercial practices. Once one realizes the extent to which the numbers taking part in an activity depend on knowledge and understanding of what is going on, it is no longer possible lightly to dismiss advertising as a means of communication. And in fact the congregation today already makes use of various types of publicity. Every month a parish letter is published, which the confirmation candidates distribute to the households in the parish. In it the most important news items concerning the congregation for the coming month are printed. For particular series of meetings, the congregation prints programmes which are distributed as widely as possible. Glass-fronted notice boards beside the church and the church hall depict the various activities, and call special attention to a particular theme in text and illustration. Finally, there are the usual announcements in the service itself, usually treated very formally.

Everyone wants to know what other people are doing and what events are taking place in their area. People feel that they have a right to information from the social institutions about their activities. The same can partly be said about the Church. In any case, people today will not become involved with the congregation or the faith without at least a superficial knowledge of the type of church activities and the content of faith. Because of this, the old form of simple announcement must be complemented by a brief, concrete outline which will enable the reader or listener to develop his own ideas.

The parish letter is an example that reveals the type of difficulties facing any kind of publicity which attempts not only to advertise but also to provide useful information. It is important first to ask exactly who reads the parish newsletter, and who should read it. It is all too easy to make too high an estimate of the readers' standard of education and understanding of the faith, with the result that no communication takes place. The impression that one wishes to convey must be attuned to the recipients' own questions. One can convey information only where the recipient feels a need for clarification. If the parish newsletter were composed to fit in with the wishes of the congregation only, it would be guilty of being both unfriendly and one-sided. Finally, the outward form must make it clear that the congregation is extending an invitation and wishes to make it easier for people to join in. The invitation must not put people off by being severely formal; this will only result in their no longer having anything to do with the congregation. Every contact between men begins at an informal level and the parish newsletter should also outwardly reflect this informality.

When one assesses the needs implicit in a type of publicity which is really concerned with communication, it becomes only too obvious that the congregation always chooses the easiest path. An invitation is merely extended to the church's activities, on the assumption that people already understand the broad outline of the congregation's life and know what lies at its centre. The congregation is content to accept the fact that there are two categories of church members: the faithful few who support the congregation, and the many others who do not want to have anything to do with belief. Every dull and unfriendly announcement merely serves to confirm the outsiders' impression that the congregation is quite unconcerned whether people come or not. If the congregation refuses to take adequate trouble to form a link with people outside, then they have no grounds for complaining that most people are so indifferent.

Publicity would have some chance of success if the congregation were to practise taking the subjects of the announcements and trying to look at them in reverse. For example, instead of underlining those traditional customs which have always been valid, one should try to emphasize those passages in the Gospels from which the Christian standards of conduct first acquired their meaning. Instead of saying what the congregation expects from its members, one should speak of what the community may expect from the congregation. Instead of preserving the ideal image of a Christian who is loyal to the congregation, one could point out that a real Christian life will be discovered only by the joint effort of Christians and non-Christians.

The congregation is emerging from a past in which everyone belonged to it and all were familiar with what went on in the Church. Hence it is not surprising that the Church today hesitates to go in for publicity. This would be admitting to the general public that the time is past when general standards and church standards of conduct coincided. But it would be equally dangerous for the congregation to underestimate other people's capacity to make their own judgments. Any anxious concern on the part of the Church to act as if general church allegiance were still a reality would rightly be regarded as a lack of truthfulness.

CHAPTER 3

Towards Flexible and Independent Membership of the Congregation

MOST PEOPLE living in the parish, when they come into contact with the Church, are in a dilemma. On the one hand, they do not want to dispense with the Church, and they know that it must necessarily exist. On the other hand, they are so dissatisfied with the outward picture conveyed by the Church as an institution and by congregational life, that they want to abolish church services and activities as superfluous in daily life. The sort of congregation which is recognized as a basic and primary necessity is still not yet obvious to them, nor have they found a substitute for the ecclesiastical forms criticized.

In all this uncertainty, the congregation can help only by pointing out that the Church is in transition. The Christian faith is not seen perfect or complete in her life; however, she does not simply maintain traditional social rules in an artificial way, but attempts to understand afresh the commission on which she was founded, and to present it in social forms. When it is thus admitted that the congregation is in transition, and a fresh questioning of its commission is associated with the concept of the Church, then the apparently insoluble dilemma may be solved. For then the type of criticism which is directed at everything in the congregation and calls it all in question is much less easily justified. On the other hand, neither is the congregation helped by absolute and unconditional acceptance of all the forms of work that have come to be connected with it. Most people find it hard to associate the image of the Church with the concept of being in transition because, for them, the Church is something strong and permanent. In this view, either one can say of the Church that even this enduring institution has now, with the emergence of a new age, reached its end, or else one can say that, with its solid framework, it will surmount the present difficulties. But people find less convincing and harder to grasp the idea that the determining mark of congregation and Church is to be true, not to itself, but to the commission of Jesus, who began his work through the Church and who will complete it. However, to recognize this is the only way of distinguishing between false delay and necessary obedience, and between the right kind of patience and the search for modernity. It may seem to the observer that the congregation has at times been slow to adapt itself to alterations in the local social structure. However, a backward glance will show how the congregation has each time, in its own way, met each new requirement.

In such an assessment of the various aspects of the life of the congregation as has been made above, it is impossible to ignore the transitional situation in which the congregation is placed at the present time. To ponder, therefore, on the fact that the congregation is in transition, and to recognize the problem of linking the idea of the congregation as one of the few permanent and unchanging organizations with that of new obedience in an altered situation, do not simply involve reflection on matters of principle. The questions which arise stem from the ambiguities of congregational life itself, and demand an answer from every individual member of the congregation. The transition to which the congregation is now being subjected, and which has already been touched on at various points in the foregoing sections, may now in conclusion be given special attention under three headings.

The concept of the Church as a regional Church under the protection of the State and linked with the organs of authority in society still has force today. Although a National Church is only one of a number of possible forms of existence for the Church, the idea that Church and State are essentially associated with each other forms the accepted background for discussion about the Church. Legally speaking, the separation between Church and State was achieved long ago, but the basic conviction that Church and State are close to each other is still expressed in the Western tradition by contractual agreements in matters of cultural and social policy and in certain privileges conceded by the State to the Church as a public institution. Those who judge the present situation on the basis of the Church's earlier position have grounds for satisfaction in her continuing influence in public affairs. On the other hand, the consideration given to the Church in political matters and in her relation to the State gives increasing cause for dissatisfaction. The narrow basis of the congregations and their pattern of existence provide grounds for the suspicion that the Church is relying essentially on her bureaucratic organization and historical prestige and is building these up without taking cognizance of the situation in the local churches. People are asking how far the Church's influence in society is justified by the local churches' pattern of existence.

The regulation of relationships between Church and State has both advantages and disadvantages in the realm of social and cultural affairs and in public life generally. It has, however, a decisive effect on the work of the individual congregation. Here the relative closeness of Church and State has very dangerous results. Dependence on the concept of the regional Church gives the congregation a sense of security, even when the Church is no longer effectively reaching people in its area. Even when there is no longer any intrinsic link with the majority of people in the area, the individual congregation still sees itself as being in an unquestioned position, because of the role which the Church plays in political and public affairs. This kind of security is not, however, the same as the untroubled mind enjoined upon the believing congregation from its very beginnings. The mind without anxiety which is rooted in faith can develop solidly institutional behaviour patterns; it also definitely induces the congregation to create means of achieving cohesion and to develop institutional organizations. But the

difficulty facing the congregation today resides in the fact that it is
being forced to decide whether it will rely increasingly on its con-
solidated structure as a social institution, or whether it will expand on
the basis of that tranquility in the faith which makes it capable of
adopting a flexible attitude to its various institutional forms. The congregation must consider whether its organizations and patterns of life
are based more on the fact that society has accepted these patterns as
ecclesiastical, or whether they bear witness to that quietness of mind
which is the gift of faith alone.

Corresponding to this transition in the relation between Church and
State, and the effect that it will have on the local church, there is a
latent uncertainty in the mind of the individual Christian when he is
accounting for his membership of the local church. There is widespread
evidence as to how the individual church member struggles to accept
the patterns and norms of the congregation as something generally
recognized and natural. Mutual confirmation that one is doing nothing
but fit into an existing pattern shores up the Christian's link with the
congregation. Although, in view of the external data regarding Sunday
church attendance and actual support for church activities, it is becoming increasingly difficult for him to regard his participation as a
natural and relatively general practice, nevertheless support is still
given to such an attitude by the fact of widespread loose attachment
to the Church and the impossibility of really distinguishing the social
relationships in a large town. If general custom is increasingly advanced
as a basis for one's own standard of churchmanship, the Christian avoids
any tension which might exist between the congregation as a group and
his social environment. On the basis of this understanding of church
membership, neither has he a clear recognition of the necessity of
strengthening the Church in the eyes of the public and securing its
institutional basis, nor does he allow himself to be brought face to face
with the question of how one attains the certainty resulting from faith,
going beyond matters of custom and general practice.

While the individual member of a congregation may thus wish to
regard himself as automatically belonging to the congregation, the
pastor and his staff, by virtue of their office, have to bear the tension
between the congregation's pretensions in its area and actually keeping it together. The members of the congregation will want to avoid
this problem, since they wish to do only what is usual. And so, when a
congregation is being built up, there is often a good deal of co-operation
between the members of the congregation and the pastor, yet immediately church life, as generally understood, is established in the area,
the pastor and his staff are left to shoulder the full burden of its con-
tinuation. The fact that a pastorate has been established provides a
permanent assurance that everything in the parish will follow the
usual pattern and, because of this, everyone is glad to leave questions
of faith as far as possible to the full-time staff. The pastor and his assistants may be personally in agreement with this arrangement, even
though it places a heavy burden on them. This, however, does not solve

the problem, for it is not the personal burden borne by the parish staff which is in question, but the *raison d'être* of the congregation itself.

The strenuous efforts of individual members of the congregation still to carry on in this way in the present situation, show how far the idea of automatic and unthinking church membership has been worn away. A mere wish to conform is no longer an adequate reason for membership of the congregation. Affiliation with the congregation results from meeting the challenge of one's daily life, a challenge which is taken up in the light of faith. The congregation's support keeps the individual from losing heart over the tasks confronting him, and helps him to understand his Christian calling better. When a congregation thus awakens to a new realization of its responsibility, the tension between the congregation and its social environment is felt in the life of each individual member, and the life of the congregation increasingly grows out of the decisions which the members themselves make in this tension between the world and the Church.

The change which the congregation is experiencing today is revealed not least in the fact that it is very difficult to answer the question, 'What is the congregation for?' The Protestant population has some idea about church services, sacraments, diaconal work, and so on. However, people are unable to specify a purpose or clear direction for congregational life. This lack of clarity derives from the fact that in the past the congregation had no particular need to prove that its existence was justified. Its social composition was identical with that of the parish as a political unit. The common interests of the inhabitants of a village, small town or growing borough were largely those of the local church. The congregation was an essential centre of communal life and, just as nobody could keep aloof from the community of those living in the area, so the individual was soon taken up into the congregation before he had had time to reflect upon it. This situation was reflected in a theology that linked humanistic and nationalist ideas with the Christian faith. The question of the *raison d'être* of a particular congregation was simply not posed—because the fellowship of believers was rooted in the daily intercourse of men with one another. Today the significance of the place where one lives is much diminished, particularly in a town area, and has given way to a very different build-up of social contacts in one's private life, occupation, and membership in associations and organizations. While in a small town, people may still greet the pastor in the street, in a city parish he is largely unknown. The congregation has long since become just one more place for social intercourse, alongside many others.

Anyone who is moving from a position of anonymous church membership or anonymous church attendance towards membership of a congregational group naturally asks himself what common aims and duties hold these groups together. The vaguer the answer to the question about the meaning of congregational organization, the more limited are the possibilities for the congregation to establish communication with its environment or to spread its influence, through witness and service, beyond its own small circle. It is not enough to have a programme which as a whole seeks to combat the anonymity of present-day circumstances by building up community life; that is an inadequate goal for the congregation. Its members would then be merely attempting to restore in a small, limited area, for their own benefit, the social conditions from which they have emerged. Nor, on the other hand, can the congregation dismiss social relationships between its members as being unimportant for matters of faith; this would be attempting to continue living in ecclesiastical forms which presuppose contact and social intercourse in the place in which people live. On the contrary, the congregation must learn to find its place in today's social structure as a functional group. In this way the congregation will realize its separateness from its environment and adapt the form of its fellowship to the anonymity of social relationships. The function of the congregation as a group is to promote debate about the questions and problems that arise in the various spheres of life to which its members belong, in relation to faith and the proclamation of the Gospel, and to send them back with the answers of the Gospel in action and witness. As a functional group, the congregation must be the starting point for representative service and for promoting dialogue between belief and unbelief. It is the responsibility of the individual member to carry both into his daily life.

During this transitional period, the end of which is not yet clearly discernible, discussions about the re-organization of the congregation often emphasize two alternatives.

One group recommends an exclusive course of action. The large number of nominal church members should be forced to a decision as to how much their membership in the local congregation still means to them. Either they should act in a manner consistent with membership, or else recognize that there is really nothing of significance that retains them in the Church. In the sense of being part of the national Church, the congregation still includes almost everyone; but if nominal members were excluded, it would be possible to build up a voluntary and self-supporting congregation. In this way, the congregation could assume a manageable size and become capable of really responsible Christian life. But such a course of action would mean excluding baptized Christians who understand themselves to belong to the Church, but happen to have a completely different idea of the practice of Church membership. At the same time, the congregation as a group would be wantonly throwing away a chance of meeting people who live in the parish but are outside its social sphere.

Others say that in the present situation the most one can do is to preserve the *status quo*. As conditions become less favourable, the congregation can only carry on the struggle. They must learn to be content with little visible success, for at the present time more is not to be given them. There is much of resignation in this attitude and it is pertinent to ask whether, in showing such lack of courage, the congregation has rightly understood its task.

The alternatives between the concentration of the congregation and a broad, unspecific openness towards everyone, are only apparently incompatible. The two aspects of the work, concentration and breadth, can be combined through directing the activities of the congregation unequivocally towards equipping its members to live their faith in the world. Equipping them must have as its foundation the idea of representation. This idea alone will free one from the feeling that, as an individual or a small congregation, one can accomplish nothing. People often say, 'God is everywhere, in nature and in the spirit of man', or, by contrast, 'God does not exist, because He does not show Himself to men'. In fact God reveals Himself in the one man, Jesus, and in Him, the One Man, He is present in this world. There are many nations around the world, many groups and associations which compose the structure of society, but between them and God stands the one 'People of God'. The Christian can understand his task only in the light of this basic concept of the presence and activity of God in the world. In the equipping of the Christian, the other constant corrective must spring from a conscious 'attitude of dialogue'. This means the willingness to accept another person's questionings, needs and problems, though they are not one's own. This attitude is first revealed in the congregation when the pastor steps down as leader and speaker in the small group, and the group participants have an opportunity of expressing themselves. The attitude of dialogue spreads as each Christian learns to listen to his partner in a conversation, instead of ignoring his opinions. God does not stand apart. The way that Jesus took to men has its counterpart in men's way to him. Neither for the individual Christian nor for the congregation as a whole are there any preconditions for entering into dialogue with one's fellows. Neither a more perfect congregational structure nor a more widespread acceptance of belief can be said to be prerequisite. The Christian is taken up into God's own movement towards His world.

There is no patent formula for a radical and consistent reformation of the congregation. The congregation must examine itself critically and become aware of the problems of the world around it, so that it can give its members some insight into the involved situation and at the same time give them a new, relaxed self-confidence. This self-confidence liberates the congregation, so that it can direct all its energies towards the goal to which God wishes to lead His world.

B. AN ANALYSIS OF NOMINAL CHRISTIANITY

by

Justus Freytag

AUTHOR'S PREFACE

ANY DISCUSSION among the general public about Christian faith and the Church today reveals an attitude that draws a sharp distinction between adherence to the Church and personal living of the Christian life. This is expressed in such phrases as 'The Christian life does not consist in church-going' or 'One can be a Christian without going to church'. Behind such sentiments there lies a basic reality that deeply affects the question of the spiritual growth and mission of the Church. The vast majority of the population are nominal church members, but in fact the life of the local church goes on without much public participation. In Hamburg, for example, although 77% of the population are members of the Protestant Church, scarcely more than 10% of these church members take part in church services or other church activities. Most church members do not identify themselves with the local congregation.

Quite apart from superficial membership of the Church, however, a kind of 'general Christianity' finds expression through occasional recourse to the services of baptism, confirmation, marriage and burial, through concern for Christian education, and in certain aspects of Christian conviction. This type of Christianity contributes to social respectability. It is regarded as a part of the generally accepted ethos of society, even where a minority of the population—in Hamburg it is 16%—belongs neither to the Roman Catholic nor to the Protestant Church.

The local church, gathering together in a loosely-structured group or community those church members who are loyal, struggles hard, particularly in the urban situation, to give an intelligent meaning to church adherence as a behaviour pattern. The parish came into existence first as a local institution, but with the broadening of social relations it has lost its frame of reference in local society. Today it offers, for church allegiance, the motive of a confessing community. Loyal church membership binds together people who are determined to give corporate expression in society to their faith. It can also, however, through an emphasis on greater piety, encourage persistence in out-dated opinions about society and patterns of Christian life which the majority of church members no longer share or understand.

Naturally, there are so many positions lying between church allegiance and this 'general Christianity' that it is hard to define where one begins and the other ends. But at the outset it is worth recording that, from the standpoint of frequency and numbers, general Christianity has all the characteristics of normal social behaviour, whereas affiliation to the local church, in spite of the fact that it takes the Christian faith more seriously, bears the mark of socially divergent behaviour. It is adherence

47

to the Church which is the easier to describe and analyse as a particular attitude. With regard to this type of general Christianity which is taken as a matter of course, it is far more difficult to avoid prejudice. Loyal church membership comprises a limited social group which the observer can easily comprehend. But in the case of general Christianity, the observer's concern is with the mass of the population, among whom, on account of lack of uniformity, there can be wide variations in behaviour and conviction. In the following chapters, despite these difficulties, an attempt will be made to throw light on the motives present in general Christianity. These reflections presuppose that there are recognizable motives behind this detached relationship to the local church. The influence of faith obviously extends further into society than regular church attendance can show. To accuse the majority of nominal church members of mere thoughtlessness or indifference is not a satisfactory explanation of their divergent kinds of attitude to the Church.

In the first part, a survey of the most important of the recent empirical studies of church allegiance, and the orientation of general Christianity from a socio-historical standpoint, serve to sharpen the problem. Next, the results of exploratory interviews and of a formal interrogation will be presented. (This investigation aimed more at dealing in some depth with the issue of faith in society than at concentrating on an opinion-poll on matters of faith and the Church.) The findings will outline the image of the Church and the attitude to belief among the Protestant population, and in a second section will give an insight into the inter-related motivations leading to a confession of Christian faith. Each section reveals socio-psychological factors with which the Church must attentively reckon in dealing with its nominal membership. Consideration of the position of general Christianity includes an enquiry into our understanding of the missionary task. The concluding section once again sets forth the basic consequences for the work of the Church which arise from this phenomenon of 'general Christianity'.

Tainan, Taiwan
1967   JUSTUS FREYTAG

Church Allegiance and 'General Christianity'

I. SURVEY OF PREVIOUS INVESTIGATIONS

(a) *Case studies*

Important studies of Protestant church life and religious affiliation in Germany which have appeared in the last ten years and have used an empirical approach, all show an awareness in their point of departure that a basic cleavage exists between the Christianity of the general public and that of church allegiance.

As early as 1956, E. Reigrotzki established in a sample enquiry into participation, in the area of the Federal Republic, in the church, politics, organizations and leisure activities, that for Roman Catholics regular church attendance was normal, but that for Protestants on the other hand irregular or very infrequent attendance was the norm admitted by 70% of all Protestant church members (E. Reigrotzki: *Soziale Verflechtungen in der Bundesrepublik*, Tübingen, 1956). 'There can be no doubt, in view of this fact, that the loyalty of Roman Catholics to their Church is stronger than that of the Protestants. What this means for religious life cannot be examined here. It would be an over-hasty judgment to maintain on this evidence, without further research, the existence of weaker religious ties on the part of Protestant Christians' (*loc. cit.*, p. 22).

F. H. Tenbruck suggests a first explanation of the divergence between church allegiance and general Christianity in a study of the Protestant community in Reutlingen (F. H. Tenbruck, 'Die Kirchengemeinde in der entkirchlichten Gesellschaft', in *Soziologie der Kirchengemeinde*, ed. by D. Goldschmidt, F. Greiner and H. Schelsky, Stuttgart, 1960). He reaches the conclusion that people regard themselves as full members of the Church even if they do not participate in the local congregation. Absence from services and congregational gatherings is not accompanied in the case of church members by any uneasy conscience that they are not fulfilling their duty. On the contrary, being a Christian is not directly related to the life of the local church, and participation in the local church is not regarded as constituting the Christian life. Thus absence in no way implies denial of Church or faith; it proceeds, rather, from the individual's lowered estimation of the local congregation, in which he knows that he has the agreement of many others who also call themselves Christians. The pluralistic structure of society has broken down the pre-industrial social order, which was not divided into separate groups and spheres of living. It is this process of social diversification which has caused the change in people's attitude to church affiliation. The modern structure of society brings the individual into a hitherto unknown conflict: membership of the Church as a distinctive group competes with membership of other groups which condition the life of the individual, such as his occupation, family, circles of acquaintances, clubs, and so forth. Church members overcome this conflict by restricting their relations with the local church to a few fixed occasions, and regarding their faith as a personal and private matter. People are decreasingly conscious of any relationship with the Church as a social institution, and church allegiance as something binding upon all is losing its strength in society. The result is widespread indifference to church services and the local church, accompanied by a personal conviction that by his way of life the individual can fully comply with the demands of the Christian faith.

In a study of the Church in Schleswig-Holstein, T. Rendtorff examines both external Christianity and the inner unity of the congregation (T. Rendtorff: *Die Soziale Struktur der Gemeinde*, 1st ed., Hamburg, 1958). He stresses more strongly than F. H. Tenbruck the fact that internal church allegiance is subject to the same change noticeable in the emergence of a type of Christianity more and more loosely attached to the Church. The crisis of the contemporary church, 'when seen from the point of view of its social structure, is none other than a calling in question of all that is "churchly", from the "external" manifestations of the national church to the "inner" life of the local parish' (*op. cit.*, p. 11). Christianity divorced from the Church is to be understood as a distorted form of church affiliation which is both backward-looking and imprisoned in tradition. It takes for granted the continuing identity of Christian norms with social norms. This outlook reflects not so much a new attitude to Church and to belief as an attempt to retain in a deflated form the substance of a past Christian order of society and its values. The situation in the local church presents a similar picture. Admittedly the inner congregation has abandoned its parochial structure and turned itself into a social group. The Christian community in the context of the village, town or city area, has given way to special 'circles' concerned with the stimulation of devotion, social contacts, and works of Christian charity, and such circles increasingly represent the reality of the Church in society. But church circles are of necessity oriented inwards towards their own community. They make use of the Church's care and concern to cultivate their own small social life. If the Church wishes to enter the contemporary social environment and engage in grappling with its problems, it must abandon the idea that Christian convictions and social customs still coincide, and at the same time emerge from the isolation of church circles.

R. Köster's study of a parish in a north German city deals exclusively with church allegiance as a special mode of behaviour (R. Köster, *Die Kirchentreuen*, Stuttgart, 1959). 'The fulfilling of the norms by a small minority is of particular interest and leads one to ask how this comes about, and what sociological factors lie behind this church allegiance which diverges from the statistically more normal attitude' (*loc. cit.*, p. 4). This study takes the matter a step further in subjecting church allegiance itself to a critical analysis, instead of, as a matter of course, treating church allegiance as Christian conduct based on conviction. The study is based on the assumption, which played a part in Rendtorff's earlier exposition, that loyal church membership is to be found amongst those people whose ideas are still relatively strongly determined by the past structure of society. The fact that loyal church membership is largely made up of old people, civil servants and the middle classes—those who find themselves at a disadvantage in industrial society, compared with former times—serves to confirm this. They regard the Church as an 'institute for morals' or a 'community of goodwill'. They see it in ideal terms based either on the old authoritarian conditions when Church and State were closely linked, or on a criticism of the anonymity of modern mass society (cf. *loc. cit.*, p. 76 f.). Secondly, church allegiance can be connected with motives originating in religious and social needs which have nothing to do with the aims of the local church. The desire for social recognition by a larger group of people and by a significant social institution, as well as the need for sociability, for solemn edification and spiritual uplift, are all bound up with church allegiance. Although the local church does not regard the fulfilling of these needs as the point of its existence, it actually adjusts itself in many ways to these expectations. There thus arises a situation in which the need for social recognition, sociability and edification continues to uphold the traditional form of faith as an essential expression of what it means to be a Christian. The strong emphasis laid on participation in the local church as a norm for Christian life today leads only to a deeper cleavage between church allegiance and general Christianity. The result appears to be that in modern society the local church is no longer capable of creative change of its own accord. It has already effected a change in its function, and it is therefore understandable that the corrective should be another form of Christianity which is outside the local church.

(b) *Interpretations summarizing the evidence*

In the three studies described above, the same starting point—that of the contemporary co-existence of church allegiance and general Christianity—appears in various aspects. The dichotomy is seen as the result of the social transition from the pre-industrial order to a pluralistic society; it is understood as a challenge to the Church to abandon its traditional social forms, and is interpreted from the point of view of the new social situation in which the local church in fact already finds itself in present-day society. The questions examined receive a summarized explanation in a study by H. O. Wölber, which utilizes the results of a sample enquiry into the attitude towards religion in the Federal Republic, as exemplified by the younger generation (H. O. Wölber: *Religion ohne Entscheidung*, 1st ed., Göttingen, 1959). The representative nature of the evidence produced makes it possible to depict, in the population, the entire continuum of attitudes to religion, to Christianity, and to the Church. Of basic significance is the finding, 'The religious quest, with its longing for beliefs confirmed, exists no longer either in the Christian sense or in that of a substitute religiosity' (*loc. cit.*, p. 55). There is no definite alternative to Christianity and the Church, either in the form of political religion, or in an aesthetic or 'natural' world-view (*Weltanschauung*), or in an enthusiasm for defined truths. Rather, Christianity is present in differing degrees of depth throughout the whole population. The gradations are determined by the degree to which firm convictions or an intellectually and ideologically well-thought-out attitude to problems of ideology are taken for granted. 'A small percentage is clearly opposed to the Church and a small percentage true to the letter of the Church's teaching' (*loc. cit.*, p. 112). The vast majority of the population lie between these two extremes, regard themselves as supporting the Church, and look favourably on matters of Christian faith and church-going. This 'in-between-Church' simply spells out the fact that the local church has developed no proper pattern for a looser type of support for the Church (*loc. cit.*, p. 112). There are no forms acknowledged by the Church in which one can practise this kind of loose affiliation.

The presentation of church allegiance and general Christianity as opposites creates contrasts where in fact there are only transitions in attitudes. Such a simplified presentation reduces the various grades of affiliation to the Church into a small group of loyal church people and the large number of people who, whilst claiming to be Christians, refuse to attach themselves to the Church. Discussion and reflection are little help in bringing this 'in-between-Church', with its uncommitted Christian attitude, to a more firm position. For one cannot say that the exchange of ideas and opinions creates certainty, which is then expressed in conduct; rather is it the case that the practice of piety and habitual behaviour leads to clearer concepts and results in more strongly held convictions. The self-confident and isolated piety of the inner church group can do little to help in this process. The only behaviour pattern which the Church can offer to those whose relationship to the Christian faith is reluctantly positive is that of regular attendance at the Sunday service. Such attendance does not imply actually joining the local church fellowships, with their many meetings, but does nevertheless permit a personal encounter through the medium of the preacher. 'The Church was always as strong as the support for its services' (*loc. cit.*, p. 41). At a time when there is general assent in society to the Christian faith, but the strength of Christian convictions declines very rapidly outside the small circle of loyal church people, then the habit of regularly attending the Sunday service is the best way to hold together in one the various gradations of Christian attitude.

On the basis of the results produced by recent sociological studies on Church and religion, T. Luckmann is opposed to that understanding of the situation which takes into account only gradations in intensity of practice and conviction, ranging from church allegiance to general

Christianity (T. Luckmann, *Das Problem der Religion in der modernen Gesellschaft*, Freiburg, 1963). Tenbruck and Köster have pointed out that, as far as attitude to the Church and attendance at services are concerned, church allegiance has become the exception in modern society. Luckmann underlines this result. 'Church allegiance is based increasingly on particular rather than on general social conditions' (*loc. cit.*, p. 30). In this development there has been no question of other ideologies or systems of values pushing aside church allegiance. It is simply that the patterns of Christian behaviour offered by the local church have lost all meaning for modern man as he seeks an integrated daily life. What is surprising is not so much the drop in church allegiance, but its continuance. If church allegiance has become so marginal in society, the question arises, what religious views correspond to the general conditions of modern society? Any unprejudiced examination must concern itself with the hypothesis 'that despite the purely marginal continuance of church allegiance, despite the overpowering historical significance of the Christian Churches for the emergence of the modern world, despite the absence of a clear and tangible institutionalized opposing religion, a new and essentially non-Christian religion is emerging in modern society' (*loc. cit.*, p. 31). This new religion can no longer come to terms with the content of the traditional and institutional forms of the Church. Yet it in no way deprives them of their power; it permeates them and radically alters their meaning. This new, essentially non-Christian religion cannot therefore be said to have the traits of a 'movement', nor does it create its own institutions. This is because in the modern world the large social institutions, the political ideologies and the problems of society as a whole, subjectively regarded, seem to the individual increasingly distant and unrelated to the problems of his life. The individual finds unifying meaning for his existence in the private sphere, in conscious withdrawal from these enormous social institutions and powerful interests which, objectively, control his existence. The important, newly-emerging, religious themes concern 'private "solutions" of the conflict between the subjectively autonomous individual and his objective powerlessness in the face of the basic facts which order the conduct of his life' (*loc. cit.*, p. 68).

Modern religious themes in such a sense are sociability and emphasis on the family. In sociability, a strong impulse is at work towards self-realization and self-confirmation. The individual feels the need to experience his success, his social status and his particular private goals in the presence of others and with others. For this purpose, close contacts and continuous togetherness are needed, but always on the condition that no one attempts to interfere with another person or to commit him to anything. Sexuality and the family are raised to the level of religious themes, because they provide the individual with the simplest way of extending his existence beyond the confines of his own personality. In his relationship to his partner and to his family, the individual can overcome his isolation without having to face his dependence on the social institutions and their standards. The twin themes of sociability and family life can tolerate without difficulty some influence from the Church and a Christian vocabulary. But, under cover of superficial Christianity, they have developed into completely independent and this-worldly concepts. The modern attitude to life which thus arises has an ideological trait, because man in his individualism refuses to accept the objective autonomy of social institutions and their decisive importance for the life of every member of society. However, this attitude is more religious than ideological, because it arises from the general social conditions of today and is anchored in society as a whole. Since men tend consciously to limit themselves to the purely inner-worldly themes surrounding their private existence, and then to elevate these to the level of a religion, general Christianity tends imperceptibly to be emptied of its Christian content, until it can no longer truly be called Christian.

(c) *Results and questions*

A review of the studies in this field so far published reveals how radically the Church's situation is affected by the co-existence of special church allegiance and general attachment to the Christian faith. Any discussion of the missionary growth of the Church must come to grips with these characteristic attitudes. The conclusions which have already been reached point to the complicated conditions that prevent any over-simplified conception of the mission of the Church. It is not enough for evangelism to address 'general Christianity' merely as a product of progressive de-Christianization and secularization, and to concentrate on integrating the growing number of fringe members into existing church life and its groups. There is equally little justification for a missionary outlook which is constantly criticizing the narrowness of the Church and its isolation from the world, and in this way presents general Christianity outside the Church as the form of Christian conduct more appropriate to the openness of secular society. Thinking in simple alternatives does scant justice to the insights which the various studies have already contributed to an understanding of church loyalty and general Christian attitudes.

At the same time, these studies reveal very different emphases in their descriptions of the dynamics of the situation. All the investigations expound the problem in a similar way, and they very largely agree in their depicture of people's attitudes to the Church and Christianity. But a considerable divergence of opinions emerges in their formulation of hypotheses and conclusions, though these certainly do not attempt to forecast future developments but merely try to pursue a step further the dynamic of what is already happening. The hypothesis that a non-Christian religiosity is emerging beneath the surface of an official Christianity follows a quite different line of thought from the suggestion that the uncertainty in the 'in-between-Church' regarding Christian conduct can best be overcome by offering Sunday church attendance as a firm rule. To say that the whole Church must find new forms of life outside both conventional parish piety and general Christianity, is to give a different assessment of the dynamics of the situation from saying that participation in the common life of the local church has lost its generally binding character for Christian existence. In order to comprehend the course of events better, the treatment of contemporary problems must be accompanied by a parallel elucidation of the socio-historical origins of the dichotomy in church membership. A historical perspective enlarges the basis for an assessment of the direction in which the tension between church allegiance and general Christianity is moving.

2. CHURCH MEMBERSHIP AND STRUCTURAL CHANGES IN SOCIETY

The history of participation in the life of the Church and the individual congregation is linked closely with the history of the political order. Because the Church wishes her preaching to be a public event, it partakes of the same forms of statement and discussion which exist in the political realm of society. If the Church is a public institution, association with it will be governed by the same pattern that determines participation in other public activities. This does not mean that the Church undergoes an 'adaptation' to social conditions which would in fact be a denial of its essence. It is rather that the parallel between political forms of communication and the shape of church membership shows, on the one hand, how the Church is open to the influence of society, but, on the other, how through this openness it acquires the possibility of permeating rules of social conduct with the faith and thus altering them (cf. on the subject of adaptation. H. Schelsky, 'Ist die Dauerreflexion institutionalisierbar?', *Zeitschrift für Evang. Ethik*, 1957, Vol. 4, p. 155 f.). To discover the relation between church membership and the structure of public life, it is necessary to examine the development of the basic institutional framework of society. Ideological conflicts and new constitutions, although more widely noticed, bring about only superficial changes. Thus the stand of the Church on social problems at the beginning of the industrial revolution, or on ideological questions during the rule of National Socialism, caused many people to leave the Church but did not necessarily also alter the forms of congregational or church life. Constitutional changes in State or Church created new legal relationships, but have not yet necessarily brought a new look to the individual's participation in the political world or in his Church. The basic forms of organization in society evolve more slowly and more independently than can be reflected in the vicissitudes of political events or in legal settlements for individual institutions.

(a) *The transition from a feudal social structure to middle-class society*

In modern times the transition from a feudal social structure to a middle-class society represents a new departure, in the form of participation in political affairs. How far-reaching has been the influence of this transition can be seen from the fact that the changing interest in

5

political affairs has produced today's unquestioned division of life into 'private' and 'public' realms. In the feudal social structure only the estates of the nobility, gentry and clergy had the right and duty to attend to public affairs. They were neither the delegates of an institution nor representatives of the population of a particular area. The prince embodied in his person the State, the gentry embodied the population of a country, and the clergy the Church as an institution. The idea that a small group of persons can publicly represent the private interests of a large number of people, and must consequently consider their interests in the exercise of office, was unthinkable in feudal society. The participation of the populace in public affairs was limited to the estates demonstrating before the public the higher power which they represented (cf. on this whole section, J. Habermas, *Strukturwandel der Öffentlichkeit*, Neuwied, 1962). Under these social conditions the corresponding actuality of Church and congregation consisted in the ministry, the church building, the traditional liturgy and the proclamation of true doctrine, for which the minister was responsible. The question of participation in church life did not yet appear as of any moment. Of course the congregation met for Sunday service, and in those days too an empty church was an occasion for complaints about the lack of piety. But it was more a question of the service being conducted by the pastor before the people, rather than of all those present celebrating the service together. What took place in church was aimed at conveying a solemn and instructive impression to the people attending, and for this reason, as far as its inner tension was concerned, it mattered less who was present at the service at any given time. The visible portrayal of the Church in liturgy and doctrine stood in the foreground.

(b) *Private piety and public participation in church affairs in middle-class society*

A middle-class society comes into existence at the moment when increasing general and public interest in matters arising from the private goals of citizens is no longer governed solely by those in authority, but the citizens themselves learn to accept these interests as their own affair. The polarity between private life and public realm which thus emerges can already be seen in the dissolution of the authority of the estates. In addition to the sovereign and his entourage, the public institutions of civil administration, the military power and the law courts acquire an independent influence. The gentry hand over their political functions to the parliamentary bodies and the lower judicature, and flock into the various professions and new occupations now opening up. The establishment of religious liberty secures for faith the character of a personal confession over against the institutional Church. The new division of life into private and public spheres is, however, based primarily on the fact that the economy of the individual household becomes the very basis of existence for the educated and active strata of society. The head of the household was faced with the necessity of checking the expenses of the household and ensuring the

profitability of its economic endeavours. It very soon proved that such
economic activity depended on a market and exchange of wares super-
vised and regulated by the authorities. The conditions governing
private economic activity extended far beyond the sphere of the individual household. The matters of public interest which first and most
closely concerned the citizens were public regulations limiting and
influencing private economic activity. By discussing them publicly and,
with the help of the press, bringing public opinion to bear, the citizens
fought the authorities for the right to be heard on these questions
affecting them all. The new political order is founded on two opposing
spheres of life. The private sphere, which includes family and profession, offers a basis for the independence of the citizen in his way of life
and his opinions. It opens up the possibility of an intimate family life,
of an individual education and of the development of personality.
Public affairs mean political discussion between private individuals,
which both provides an opportunity for reasonable settlement of differing opinions and, in the form of public opinion, limits the power of
the administrative state and of social institutions. The supporting
elements in middle-class society, composed in the beginning of the
merchants, entrepreneurs, civil servants, professional men, teachers,
army officers and government office workers, were convinced that they
could retain autonomy in their private lives solely by taking part in
critical public discussion, and that the only person who could expect
to obtain a public hearing was the one who could show evidence that
his private life was free and independent.

The awakened private interest of middle-class society in the problems
of the community also moulded conscious affiliation to the Church.
Faith and devotion were, to begin with, taken into the private sphere
which was then opening up. In addition to the Church, the pastor's
ministry and Sunday church attendance, a new place of devotion
emerged in the middle-class home, uniting the members of the family.
The church building was no longer the only place where services were
held. Worship at home, led by the father, acquired an important place
on significant family occasions and major church festivals, and through
the habit of household devotions, there was an increase of family Bible
reading and prayers. One can explain the growth in private devotional
practice only by a more personal understanding of faith, which itself
developed from the concept of individual responsibility for the conduct
of one's life and of a closer and more intimate relationship between
members of the family within the home. Faith is now expected to have
significance in the formation of personality and in the performance of
family and professional duties. Confessing the faith no longer means
the acceptance of dogma and church doctrine. It is seen rather as something growing from independent judgment and inner consent to
Christian assertions. Only an independent and personally responsible
expression of conviction can awaken faith, either between men of
equally independent powers of judgment or in the close relations existing between parents and children. This new, ethical-rational and

inward understanding of faith forms the basis for the domestic practice of piety and for the discussion of Christian topics.

With this private piety was associated a new form of independent participation in the Church's public affairs. The Church is now represented by the cohesion of the congregation rather than by the pastoral office, Christian doctrine and services held in church buildings. In the local area of the parish, the new middle classes also take up church affairs as matters of public concern. They wish to see their private opinions receiving consideration, and not to have matters decided simply by the church authorities. Debates about varying doctrinal tendencies or forms of service awaken public opinion. Different viewpoints are mostly aroused on matters like the conduct of the pastoral office or the appointment of a new minister. Endowments, donations and contributions to the Church, which, in the train of economic development, is increasingly unable to exist on its own resources, show how influential citizens support the work of the local church out of their interest as private individuals. The growth of public opinion on church affairs and a willingness to take on financial responsibility give a new significance to the office of church-warden or elder, which is now assumed by prominent citizens. Moreover, the personal understanding of faith, originating in private life, introduces to the Church as a public institution new areas of Christian activity in charitable works and education, for which the upper layers of the middle class feel personal responsibility and in which, as church members, they assume honorary functions. As long as the established Church offered no scope for awakened private interest, this expressed itself in Christian voluntary associations, societies, and special circles outside the Church. But these free Christian associations for the renewal of piety soon became part of ordinary church life.

The local congregation now emerged as a social unit manifesting the Church in society. Amongst the causative factors were discussions conducted among church members in the parish, relying on their own judgment; co-operation in new tasks for the Church defined according to the individual's independent understanding of the faith; and the readiness of individuals to bear financial responsibility for the Church's work. If there is today a call for a visible, unified, local church structure, for regular meetings to hear the Word proclaimed and to talk about issues of faith, and for independent co-operation and shared responsibility among members of the congregation, it is because of the normative effect of this form of participation in public and church life, which has become an accepted part of middle-class society. The participation of middle-class society in church life is independent and responsible, because it is rooted in the piety practised in the private sphere of home and occupation, and in the convictions there acquired. Interest in biblical proclamation and faith is continuous, because it is embedded in the public life of the local community. The ongoing exchange of judgments and opinions between prominent private individuals in local society also includes their attitude to Church and faith.

(c) *Church membership in the re-politicized social sphere*

The extent to which the middle-class way of life and its ideals found acceptance in the broader sections of the population caused a further shift in the political order. The separation between private and public life, for which the middle classes had fought, gave way before a single 're-politicized social sphere', in which industrial firms, occupational organizations, big associations, political parties and state administration all in like manner, out of concern for the interests of the individual citizen, legitimized themselves and made their own particular ends into public concerns (cf. J. Habermas, *loc. cit.*, p. 194 f.). This development was under way from the moment the economically weaker groups in society, in order to achieve the same independence and autonomy as the middle classes, succeeded in getting state support for their economic interests. The further the State went in meeting these expectations with redistribution of income, subsidies and communal welfare activities— and subsequently the further industrial enterprises went in providing the employee with social security, the chance of social advancement and more personal atmosphere in his place of work—the more an outwardly middle-class citizenship spread through the population. But the price paid for this was that home and occupation no longer formed the centre for independent economic action. Whereas the private autonomy of the family was formerly rooted in its function as an economic unit, it now focuses on! the function of consumption. Together with this shift, however, has come a massive incursion into private life by the advertising pressure exercised by semi-public institutions, which conditions the use of leisure time. During this same period, public discussion of issues arising from private life, which the people themselves take up against the authority of the State and traditional institutions, has increased by leaps and bounds. Wider and wider circles of the population are taking part in this debate, and it continues to grow in extent. Book publishers, the press, films, radio and television act as purveyors and supporters of different opinions, judgments and ideas. Publishers popularize the middle-class novel, the press presents political events for the widest possible circle of readers, the mass media bring culture and political events close, and as they do so, economic considerations always play a part. However, with this broadening and commercialization, active public discussion changes into consumer behaviour. The critical public disintegrates into the large number of merely receptive consumers, on the one hand, and the few specialists on the other who no longer debate publicly. As a consequence, the subjects which move the public come less and less frequently from the middle-class strata whose private views are being affected, but are placed before the public by the social institutions of the associations, industry and the State.

In the re-politicized social sphere the individual can only with difficulty escape public influences. They are present as much at home and in his leisure time, through the offers of the consumer market, as at his place of work and in every form of social intercourse and conversation.

The problem of a special concern for public affairs, arising from within the independent economic unit of the middle-class home, can therefore hardly be said to exist any more. The pressures of publicity exerted by public institutions so permeate the life of society that the individual gets the impression that all his needs are already provided for. When he reflects about his personal interests, he can obviously, from among the rival offers put before him, choose this or that opinion, but he strongly suspects that he is only changing from one sphere of social influence to another. The experience of disillusionment which clings to this uncertainty creates suspicion and enmity towards social institutions as a whole.

The situation of a person who, through his occupation, background or career has a close connection with one of the social organizations is different. When he observes what is taking place in his organization and in society generally, he will understand that in the present political order, the important formation of opinion and significant balancing of interests take place at the level of the various organizations and the state administration. This insight, even though perhaps incompletely realized, can in any case motivate him to maintain formal participation in the organization. If the individual member becomes consciously aware of how public events are actually moving, he will bring his own opinions critically to bear within the organization's own affairs. The limited audience within the organization gives his voice a certain weight, and working in this restricted public sphere, the individual can penetrate further into the process of decision-making than he could with any engagement in general public debate.

One cannot say that the Church has extended any special publicity from the top downwards among the public at large. Nevertheless the two model attitudes towards participation in public affairs in contemporary society can also at any given moment be seen in relation to faith and the Church. The direction of development does not point only to a congregation which comprises a particular social group in society. Of course this change is very obvious. It began to take effect when the spread of public discussion, both geographically and socially, broke apart the web of communication which the middle class had possessed in local political life. With the dissolution of social contacts between private individuals, from which public opinion originally received its critical impulse and direction, continuing interest in the local church was weakened and its affairs were no longer regarded as of public concern. Private devotion and personal understanding of the faith, which once set the pace for the established Church and found their independent expression in the intimacy of the middle-class home, now leans largely on the institutional group life of the congregation. The local church gathers a circle of persons who wish to be Christians in a devoted way and makes them a 'family'. At the end of this process there emerges the image of an inward-looking group-public, which encourages active participation only by those who are in one way or another already participating members.

Parallel with this, however, an opposite tendency makes itself felt. For many church members, reaching one's own insight and personal conviction in matters of faith was more important than the fellowship of the local church, and they attempted to carry on a kind of personal and domestic piety even without the basis of a separated private sphere. The simple fact that increasing numbers of the population were externally adopting middle-class ways of life kept alive this tendency to private devotion, together with the ideals of intimacy and personal education. Significantly, therefore, people still make use of the Church for private events in the family and for the Christian education of young people, and maintain their limited financial support, but apart from this exercise no influence on what happens in the local church. The ethically orientated understanding of faith, with its emphasis on personal insight, which was once linked with middle-class family life, also retains its normative influence in general Christianity. In place of the private sphere, journalism and literature now serve to promulgate this attitude of responsibility. As institutional pillars of extended public opinion, they continue in the religious field the tradition of middle-class criticism of the established authorities. From its beginnings the tendency towards private devotion concentrated on the problem of a personal and honest faith, whereas the local church became increasingly concerned with questions of community and church organization. When the Church did develop publicity, it did so in a way which intentionally overlooked the tension between the direction of private Christianity and the ideas in the local church. Such a form of publicity, which ignored these differences, was likely to strengthen the impression in the public mind that the Church, like other social institutions, merely wanted to make sure of retaining its members. Because of this impression, the majority of people came in due course to feel the same distrust for the Church as they did for any other social organizations which advertise, without being able to formulate their own attitude to faith.

In this brief comparison between the changes in political forms of communication and in patterns of church membership, as they have developed out of the feudal social structure, via middle-class society, into the present type of abstract public sphere created by the social institutions, a two-fold process is revealed. The decisive dynamic of the situation focuses in two issues: first, whether general Christianity is growing further and further away from any relation to faith and any actual dispute about its content, and secondly, whether the local church, resting on the esteem which it once enjoyed in a previous epoch as the upholder of public concerns, is today merely aiming at creating an intimate community life that will win members while avoiding any discussion or clash of opinions. In the former case, it is a question of the importance of the content of faith for an understanding of one's own experience. In the latter, it is the Church's task which is at stake; since middle-class life no longer provides it with a basis for activity, the local church should at least try to create an internal public that will comprise as many divergent opinions as possible.

The socio-historical point of view also reveals the fact that nominal Christianity and church allegiance are more closely connected than at first appears. Both these relationships to faith have developed in a parallel way, and arise from the new and deeper attitude to the Church which middle-class society sought to reach. The desire to profess the faith from an inward conviction and free insight, and recognition of the need for Christian responsibility in public life, both stand out clearly. When middle-class public life and the field of local politics began to lose their influence, the two impulses continued to be effective in different patterns of social conduct, but nevertheless remained essentially related to one another. It is only when outside social pressures increasingly destroy the independence of the private sphere, and the advertising methods of social institutions blunt the edge of public discussion, that there is an ambiguity which, with regard to general Christianity, will be the object of further investigation (cf. on the situation of the local church, the preceding study by K. Ozaki).

3. THE PROBLEMS TO BE EXAMINED

The processes at work in general Christianity cannot be comprehended if they are understood in terms of participation or non-participation in the local church. This has been indicated in the summary of previous investigations, and our socio-historical survey has established this result more firmly. In face of the attempt among Christians in general to master their own questions about life independently in a personally acquired faith, the problems of the Church take second place. When the individual is faced with church affairs, he finds that these problems tie him to lines of thought about belief which run right across his own expectations and his own conception of faith. His reflections run in the direction of 'What does belief mean to me?', and not 'What kind of recognition and what kind of commitment does the Church deserve from me?' In general Christianity, the decision does not concern a particular degree of participation in the life of the local church, but depends on the question how far the content of faith can elucidate divergent personal experiences, the task of leading one's own life, and concrete relations with one's fellow-men. Are Christian convictions still the material men use to explain their own experiences and personal problems, or have other unsystematic and home-made religious attitudes supplanted the content of the faith? Can one say that today general Christianity based on the faith is being displaced by a kind of religiosity which is oriented towards various ideologies, and used exclusively for individual interpretations of life?

The decision over which general Christianity is hesitating has a certain urgency in relation to the, in theory, equally important attempts to renew the life of the local church. For here it is a question of whether, outside every church activity, the biblical proclamation is not in fact already at work among men. The human contacts fostered in the local church, and the readiness for service which it can inspire, presuppose a previous encounter with faith. Of course public proclamation of the biblical message has its place in the local church, but above all the confrontation with Christian assertions takes place in the most varied ways in the actual situations of daily life and the context of traditional concepts. The personal history of an individual's wrestling with the assertions of the proclamation creates an open attitude, with which the local church and its activities can link up.

The attempt to elucidate what kind of convictions about Christian belief are present in the Protestant population faces of necessity one fundamental difficulty. The linking of general Christianity and private life—that is, one side of the polarity between the public and private realms—made it clear that there is here present an independent tradition of discussion about faith. It is different from the devotion which is fed by regular contact with a local church. In these circumstances, the realization that the proclamation that is preached and the proclamation that is heard are not identical must be applied in a broader sense. The difference between the intended content of the proclamation and the convictions which are accepted affects not only the relation between preacher and listener, but also the relation between the attempts of the Church to proclaim the gospel as a whole, and the way in which the populace adapts the proclamation to its personal creed. Of course the content of faith found in general Christianity does come from sermons and religious instruction. But it is an open question which contents and subjects take such a central place in general Christianity that they also determine what is accepted or rejected in the broader field of faith and the Church. One aim of the following investigation is to discover step by step what constitutes faith within general Christianity. To begin with, particular assertions are overlaid by opinions about the Church and an undifferentiated attitude to faith. To a certain extent, general Christianity is a criticism of church allegiance, and our investigation must take this fact into account, because it contributes to the shaping of attitudes. But only an examination of particular themes of belief can indicate what faith means for the nominal church member and whether or not it has a real function in his life. On the basis of popular understanding of the biblical proclamation and its tradition, the investigation can then deal with its other aspect, which attempts to clarify whether the religiosity that is spreading can any longer be called Christian.

This investigation seeks to discover how faith is experienced in general Christianity, and what answers men find in the Christian confession to the questions facing them in life. The enquiry is followed by the further consideration, whether faith amongst nominal church members still contributes to their understanding of their own existence, or whether attitudes other than Christian have come to take its place.

CHAPTER 2

The Presence of Faith

THE VARIOUS stages of the investigation took place in Hamburg between 1961 and 1965. A scientific working party on social research, composed of psychologists and sociologists, was responsible for the methods employed and for carrying out the enquiry. The working party had a staff of trained interviewers at its disposal. Responsibility for the thematic co-ordination of the study was in the hands of a joint committee of theologians and of the staff members of the scientific working party engaged in the study. The joint committee discussed the findings of each stage of the investigation and laid down subsequent procedure. Thus the study grew out of a continuous dialogue between theology and the social sciences.

(a) *The exploratory stage*

The evidence discovered in the first stage of exploration was based on 50 interviews with individuals, each lasting several hours. These were supplemented by four group interviews, with an average of five participants in each. The scientifically-qualified members of the working party themselves carried through this research. The persons interviewed in these exploratory enquiries were adults from various social classes. The majority were middle-aged and were only nominal church members. Particular interest was paid to those church members who take no part in the services or other activities of the local church.

The exploratory enquiry can be described as a free conversation between the interviewer and the person being interviewed (respondent) (cf. the section in the appendix entitled 'Explanation of the Methods Employed'). The interviewer enters into the conversation with only a list of subjects as a guide. He starts the conversation with some provocative questions, and follows up those opinions expressed which are of special interest for the investigation. His task is to listen carefully, and to create a situation in which the respondent can speak freely and without embarrassment, rather than to ask questions all the time himself. As a method, the exploratory enquiry makes it possible to clarify the viewpoints to be investigated, without pursuing the problems by questioning. The rather free nature of the dialogue avoids any danger of putting questions to people that are so far removed from their own way of thinking that they do not concern them. The respondent decides the way the argument goes, so that the interviewer can analyse the reasons and explanations put forward and recognize the underlying motivations.

The exploratory enquiry was concentrated on the following areas:

1. Expectations in relation to the faith.
2. Attitudes to the Church.
3. Assessment of the Church's 'contribution' in preaching, liturgy and teaching.

The conversations intentionally covered a wide range of subjects, in order to search into the motives which guide general Christianity.

The first psychological survey of the evidence revealed how difficult it is in conversation to get down to the level of making a declaration of faith. Even among people with limited knowledge, there was a great need to speak in general terms about belief; and people were very ready to discuss the Church, even though they themselves took no part in it. This situation raised the question, What kindled this eagerness to enter into the conversation and to join in passing judgment? Indeed the readiness to subject views and social institutions to criticism predominated so strongly that the dimension of personal conviction played only a limited part in the talks.

(b) *The stage of investigations prior to using measurement techniques*

To break through the general talk on faith and the Church, the Analysis of Meaning method was now used (cf. Appendix 1, Explanation of the Methods Employed). The fresh series of interviews related to a list of key words designed to test the emotional background of this discussion on faith and the Church. The list of words included:

1. (a) *security*	2. (a) *trust*	3. (a) *knowledge*	4. (a) *responsibility*
(b) *certainty*	(b) *belief*	(b) *truth*	(b) *obedience*
5. (a) *mankind*	6. (a) *failure*	7. (a) *morals*	
(b) *neighbour*	(b) *guilt*	(b) *challenge*	
		(c) *commandment*	
8. (a) *meaning*	9. (a) *anxiety*		
(b) *aim*	(b) *death*		
(c) *hope*			
(d) *expectation*			

The associations of ideas with these terms showed that the respondents attached nothing personal to most of the terms, and indeed that many of the words seemed to them to belong to a language that was out-of-date. Personal experiences and daily happenings did come into play with the words *security, responsibility, neighbour* and *failure*. But the respondents drew no connection between these terms and the assertions of the faith which relate to them. The words unlocked their own experiences in the area of their families, and (in part) of their occupations. If their attention was drawn to the relation of the words to faith and the Church, then they immediately thought of what the terms meant for the conduct of the Church in society; they reproached the Church with these words. Only secondarily did they remember what the Church says in its proclamation in regard to the facts signified by these expressions. The feelings and qualities of experience in which talk about faith is rooted can best be grasped in the word-cluster, *belief, knowledge, meaning, aim, hope* and *expectation*. At the same time the terms *aim* and *expectation* reflect a tension which is deeply felt, even in daily life, while the words *faith, knowledge, meaning* and *hope* point to a more general tension which, however, because it reaches so much further, releases weaker associations of ideas. The tendency to consider things in a detached way, oriented towards the social environment only, is also operative here.

The next step in the investigation was intended to throw light on the content of experience associated with the terms *knowledge, meaning* and *hope*, and to find out the function of belief in this connection. The enquiries were centred round the subjects:

1. *Meaning of life*
2. *Transitory nature of life*
3. *Threat of death*
4. *Function of faith as consolation and as encouragement to act.*

These themes caused the respondents to speak very personally, and to produce a mass of situations and reflections from their own lives. In replying, the partners in the dialogue described the type of reaction which they themselves had developed and employed in their own experiences. They very seldom paid any attention to the more fundamental consideration, whether they had done justice to the demands of the situation through this type of behaviour. The many different kinds of personal experience produced, which were impossible to reduce to any system, as well as the fact that answers related essentially to the lives of individuals, showed that the possibilities of the exploratory enquiry as a method were exhausted.

Forty interviews were conducted for the Analysis of Meaning, and the exploration of the subjects *Meaning of life, hope* and *faith* further comprised detailed conversations with 30 people.

(c) *The stage of measurement assessment*

In exploratory enquiries the assessment of the results by the interviewer has a great influence. Without a clear judgment on the answers, aided by psychological and sociological models, the material would have only a random, biographical character. For this reason the investigation included statistical processing of the survey material. The results can in this case be quantified.

The interpretation of the quantified material is determined much more by the reaction of the respondents. All the answers of the respondents are included on an equal footing in the analysis. In reporting an exploratory enquiry, the interviewer must necessarily himself decide what is important or unimportant in the opinions expressed. Mathematical handling of the data makes it possible to discover which answers the respondents on their part consider to be of equal importance. The decision as to which answers are to be included no longer rests with the interpreter, on the basis of his intuition or social experience, as in the case of the exploratory enquiry. Statistical processing ensures that the problems uncovered in the exploratory enquiry are interpreted in accordance with the views and opinions of the persons being interviewed.

A formal interrogation brought together in short provocative propositions the positions which had emerged from the personal reports in the last exploratory stage and also from the statements reported in the preceding investigations (see Appendix 2, Table of Statements). At the same time, care was taken to balance the negative and positive statements regarding the faith. The persons chosen to be interviewed in this formal survey had to give their views on these short propositions, which were formulated as general statements, without digressing into the sphere of personal experience. The statements related to the following questions:

> *the meaning of life*
> *the transitory nature of life*
> *general and specific anxiety*
> *the threat of death*
> *loving one's neighbour*
> *the individual and the actions of God*
> *the individual and the actions of Jesus Christ*
> *the Church and its services, baptism in particular.*

The interview form consisted of 111 statements about faith and additional, supplementary questions about the individual, his social circumstances and his relationship to the Church. The interrogation, which on an average took 1½ hours, was applied to 100 adults. To test the list of statements and the method, a further 40 persons were involved in preliminary tests. In order to make the factor of conscious affiliation to the Church stand out with sufficient sharpness, the choice of persons for the formal interrogation was made in such a way that one half of those questioned were church-goers, in the sense that they attended at least once a month, and the other half were nominal church members who did not attend services. The composition of the sample was also related to the pattern of sex, age, social class and family position in the total population. In the church-going category, however, the special structure of the congregation according to social class and average age was also noted. In this way an approximately representative cross-section of opinions could be attained (see Appendix 3, Demographic Characteristics of the Respondents in the Formal Interrogation). The interrogations were carried out by a staff of experienced interviewers.

Evaluation of the results was done in two stages. First, the various answers were reduced to percentages. But it was very quickly plain that a simple percentage reckoning of the numbers who accepted or rejected the respective statements, in relation to the number of persons interviewed, was not sufficient for the classification of the whole mass of material. The very detailed interview form allowed too many different interpretations. Therefore as a second step, a factor analysis was used on the results obtained: a method of measuring which correlated each answer of any individual with all his other answers, and also with those of all other persons interviewed. Using this factor analysis, it was possible to work out a small number of definite and independent factors for the problems outlined in the statements (see, on factor analysis, Appendix 1). For this an electronic computer was used. These factors, being leading terms produced from the data themselves, reflect the respondents' real opinions and motives on the subjects of the interrogation.

The transition to formal interviews based on the table of statements led the investigation decisively away from the survey of detached discussions and personal reports. The people interviewed were offered different competing interpretations of the problems they felt concretely. Under the pressure of having to decide on one meaning or another, it was possible to perceive the direction in which the respondent's own method of overcoming the problem was running. Since the interrogation covered not only the subjects of the last stage of the exploratory enquiry but also the subjects used at the beginning, the insights from all the exploratory surveys could be tested again with a larger unit of respondents.

2. ATTITUDE TO THE CHURCH

(a) The Church as a bureaucratic organization

At first glance, the Church appears to people to be a bureaucratic organization. Like the State, government agencies, political parties, trade unions, and the great interest groups, the Church also has its place as one of the social organizations. Like other administrative and unifying organizations which are important to society, the Church is regarded as something that exists as a matter of course, the non-existence of which it is difficult to conceive.

It would be inaccurate to imply that this impression of something bureaucratic has been created by concrete experiences which the individual church member has had with the local church or pastor. Today it is popular to point out that a national Church, where most members of society are included as members of the Church, has a particular tendency to develop the characteristics of a bureaucratic organization. Since the Church's aim to integrate all baptized members in the local church, and also to give guidance in socio-political issues, far exceeds its ability to fulfil these things in practice, it is understandable if the Church, in order to do anything at all, often withdraws into behaviour characteristic of a bureaucratic organization. The pattern of occasional offices, stretching from baptism through confirmation and marriage to burial, and the Church's public statements, all exhibit the characteristics of 'administrative solutions'. In conceiving the Church as an organization, people are giving neither a positive nor a negative answer to this question of whether the Church has become congealed in a mould of rigid, systematized rules governing its activities. The Church is rather regarded by the populace as a bureaucratic organization because it has certain tasks to perform for the whole of society.

> 'The Church is mixed up in public administration, such as film censorship, but no one knows exactly how far.'

Most people are unable to give more accurate expression to the tasks the Church performs for society. Most would also have difficulty in being specific as regards the bureaucratic apparatus of State, parties and interest groups, and could not easily say why they are necessary for the whole of society or what function they have for community life. As far as the Church is concerned, if people reflect upon its contribution to the whole, they would probably reply in terms such as these: it ought to give people inner conviction to prevent them from drifting; it ought to stand up for moral standards in a way the state cannot (cf. G. Kehrer, 'Religiöse Praxis und Religiöses Bewusstsein: Material zur Kritik der Säkularisierungsthese', Bericht no. 2 in the series *Studien und Berichte aus dem Soziologischen Seminar der Universität Tübingen*, 1963/64, p. 20). But if one rates the Church as a bureaucratic organization, it makes exactly this kind of more extensive reflection unnecessary. Once the Church is recognized as an institution pervading the whole of society, it must then have tasks which the individual cannot grasp in detail and does not need to understand completely.

Curiously enough, it does not occur to people that the Church could be a special community, or that it represents particular opinions that differ from the convictions of the majority. If the vast majority of the population, across all social levels and differentiations, belongs to the Church, taking it quite superficially it is difficult to regard the Church as a particular group of people. The community idea founders, because of the completely detached relationship to the Church which is prevalent. In addition there is the fact that for many people the term 'community' has completely negative connotations, inherited from the National Socialist period. To speak of the Church as a community is automatically to speak of it in a derogatory fashion.

> 'Religious community? This is just an expression from the income tax form. There isn't any community any more. We're still fed up to the back teeth with the idea of a "National Community". Today everyone must see how he can manage on his own: leave others in peace, and be left in peace himself.'

The same applies to any image of the Church which tries to bring into the foreground the particular views of Christianity. Membership of the Church being so widespread, the only man who can recognize one particular opinion as binding is one who has committed himself to a general and binding philosophy. Such an outlook would enable him to distinguish between convinced Christians and half Christians, between the beliefs of Christianity and personal opinions. Only a few people adopt a definite standpoint of this kind, and experience with political ideologies in the past has bred a scepticism which makes people wary of definite convictions and ideologies. As a result of the relativization of traditional values and ethical appeals, general philosophies no longer seem so important, and people regard the Church in a way that shows little concern for particular Christian opinions.

'Values and morals are the postulates erected in previous ages which were and are so often broken by the people at the top and by ourselves too. They are still perhaps something worth aiming at, but today we are farther away from them than ever.'

(b) *Criticism of the Church*

If the Church is understood more or less as a matter of course as a bureaucratic organization, this does not in any way mean that people are not critical of it. Just because it counts as one of the large social institutions the public judges it very critically, and some of the criticism of the Church is perhaps the strongest proof of the thoughtless way in which a vague concept of the Church's function in society as a whole is regarded as its essential task. This very widespread critical attitude can well be demonstrated even from the reactions of the respondents to the interviews and their subject matter:

'It is high time the Church showed some concern for what is really wrong with its "sheep", instead of the pastors just sitting there and preaching. What they say has nothing to do with today, and no one understands it anyway.'

In the opinion of the broad mass of the population, the Church possesses no recognizable or visible power. It does not look active or dynamic; rather it seems to be tired and weak. Its attempts to co-operate in social and cultural problems are felt to be misdirected as well as half-hearted. In this sphere the Church comes into competition with the State welfare institutions, trade unions, political parties and so forth, all of which have a better bureaucratic organization and stronger finances. In their judgment of the Church's influence, men form their opinions from outward impressions, and Protestants often draw comparisons with the Roman Catholic Church, which is more successful in getting its way with the State.

'The Church looks like an old firm that can no longer keep up with the times.'
'You can tell it from politics; the Catholic politicians stand together and are supported by their Church down to the last village priest. The Protestant politicians take swipes at each other, and the Church couldn't care less about politics. It is content if it gets its church tax.'

But even within its own province, the proclamation of the Gospel, there is a feeling that the Church is disunited and uncertain. It seems itself to be divided in matters of faith, and to be living in a continual crisis. People miss a responsible spiritual centre and an absolutely valid authority in the Church, and wish that at least here in ideological matters an unequivocal position could be presented.

'Some pastors say the kingdom of God will come just like it says in the Bible, and others say these words are only symbols, and if you're uncertain, all they can say is, "You have to have faith" and they can't help you.'

'Then there's Niemöller, and then there's Dibelius, and they say quite contradictory things in public.'

'Some pastors talk directly about the devil and the good Lord, so that you can imagine one with horns and the other with a beard, and then you have someone like Professor Thielicke, whose preaching is completely modern and up-to-date.'

For someone who is uncertain and has doubts, the local church does not look sufficiently impressive or have enough prestige for him to be able to identify himself with it. When it is a question of turning to the Church, the general opinion is that the encouragement is lacking which would otherwise be derived from the fact that people who are respected and socially well regarded support the Church. There is a general readiness today to admit that even the most able and successful people also have to grapple with doubts and questions. If these people do not go to church, then Christianity can give no answer to one's own lack of certainty.

'Anyone who believes that and follows it (what the Church represents) is a poor fool.'

'Church-going has gone completely out of fashion. Previously one didn't dare not to go on Sundays. Today you're noticed if you do go.'

'The Church does not help you if you're in doubt; it just leaves you to your doubts. It doesn't lead to belief, it is only approachable if you have overcome your doubts and already believe.'

Finally, there is the widespread opinion that the Church has failed historically. This concerns the two great turning points of recent history, the First World War and the National Socialist period. It is believed that in both cases the Church did not speak out unequivocally about wrong, but made compromises with nationalism.

'Despite the commandment "Thou shalt not kill", the nation's soldiers were blessed by the Churches so that they would kill the enemy.'

'The Church is supposed to represent world-wide Christianity, to be as it were a world organization, but in fact in every country it is just an appendage to the national state bureaucracy.'

'There was a fighting Church which opposed the Hitler regime, and there were pastors who put on the brown shirt immediately after their sermon, and both were acting in the name of God.'

Social influence, ideological authority, social prestige and the attitude in times of national crisis in the past, are all discussion points which play a part in people's judgment of the vast social organizations such

6

as the traditional political parties, the big associations and cultural institutions, as well as in their criticism of the Church. It is to be supposed that the popular objections to the other large bureaucratic organizations are largely similar, *mutatis mutandis*, to the pattern of criticism of the Church. These objections arise from an attitude which, at a great distance from what really happens in these organizations, enjoys holding a mirror up to them from the viewpoint of the man in the street.

This kind of criticism is more difficult to indulge in, the moment the particular purpose of the organization comes into focus more clearly. As far as the Church is concerned, there is a contradiction between its local church work, which only reaches a small number of people, and its character as an institution embracing the whole of society. The fellowship in the local church does not fit into the image of the Church as a bureaucratic organization. The contradiction is generally solved by separating the local congregation from the Church. The local church exists in an enclave from which the public are excluded. It is for old people and children, the unfulfilled and the weak. In addition, it is affected by the same uncertainty and criticism of faith as exists outside, and an exposition of the Bible which is arbitrary and lacking in unanimity helps churchgoers no further forward. The vast majority of the populace refuses to regard the local church as anything like what the Church ought to be.

'The local church can't help a doubter, because you almost have the impression that they can't even help themselves today. And then the pastor stands up in the church and preaches as if he knew nothing about this and had only strongly convinced hearers in front of him. But who are the congregation today? Old people, children who have to go because they are being prepared for confirmation, and weaklings. That is what the congregation looks like today. Even if one really wants to go, as an adult who has a life to live, one is embarrassed at the idea of belonging to it today.'

(c) *The Church as a non-temporal institution*

Parallel to the attitude which regards the Church as a bureaucratic organization, there is a second attitude to the Church more strongly motivated by the individual's own fears and questionings. Here one finds the conviction that the Church must be something other than a purely temporal institution which is exclusively concerned with its power and public image. It is held that the Church must from its very nature stand apart from contemporary public debates and discussions. If man easily loses his direction in today's world, and is almost obliged to act in ways which he cannot reconcile with his conscience and which he will probably later regret, then the Church should not form part of this daily life which is based on compromises, ambition and business. The Church is based on a few timeless truths which are valid beyond and apart from the conflict of opinions. It is regarded as a non-temporal reality, which cannot be described by categories taken from the social environment:

'Behind the Church there stands the institution which created the world and which guides world history.'

'It is an impressive thought, and it inspires reverence, it strikes you when you see the enormous old church buildings, to think that the Church has existed for centuries, has outlasted all forms of State, and even in Russia cannot be extinguished.'

'When he isn't there, you can smile about the pastor, as you might about a teacher, but when you actually meet him, it is rather different. You don't like to say to him that you don't believe. You're with someone of whom you know that he is a believer, and in a certain sense God's representative, and you respect him so much that you can't just tell him openly why you don't believe, like you would with a friend.'

The reverence and respect for a greatness behind the Church, which is more felt than understood, cannot be said to be based on the actual impression made by the church building, the pastor or the church service, but rather is read into the Church. The Church is given the role of taking a counter-position to all rapid change, contradictory ideas and relativism; a position which it is in fact as a social institution incapable of fulfilling. Between the image of the Church as a non-temporal institution and its practical activity in the local church, there is at least as great a difference as there is between the understanding of the Church as a bureaucratic organization and its actual influence on society as a whole. In an attempt to skirt the question of belief, the individual transfers directly to the Church the point of view that there must necessarily be something timeless and permanent.

(d) *Preaching, the pastoral office and occasional services*

Nevertheless the concept of a difference in kind is more particularly applied to preaching, the pastoral office and occasional services, and not only to an undefined function of the Church in society as a whole. The sermon especially, the conduct of the pastoral office, and the occasional services are judged by the feeling that the Church must be something non-temporal, and in this kind of judgment the individual is deeply involved. The Sunday service is there to strengthen faith and Christian conviction. It should help to quell the doubts which arise for contemporary man from science and from confrontation with non-Christian attitudes. If contemporary manifestations of indifference and apathy threaten every deep conviction, the point of a service is to restore one's faith. Church attendance could be some help if one could thereby once more attain a conviction and certainty in the basic elements of faith. But instead, the sermon in fact just throws up more questions and doubts, because it generally discusses the most difficult elements of faith. The sermon is interesting only for Christians who are advanced in the faith, and offers too little for those who with simple and unchanging expectations are hoping for a firm belief.

'Once a year at Easter you hear something about the resurrection, and the creed has something about eternal life. Instead of this you have sermons on any old theme [referring to the Sunday lessons] which mostly don't apply to you. This bores me and doesn't help me. Protestant teaching should place far greater emphasis on its great themes [meaning redemption, resurrection, the last judgment and eternal life].'

In an age which hardly recognizes human example any longer, and leaves little space for personal encounter, the pastor should be no ordinary official or academic person. The office of the pastor embodies the eternal and the timeless, and on the basis of his commission he must, through his example, make the ideals visible in all spheres of life. For him firm belief must make possible a personal attitude which can give an example to all, and has the power to radiate conviction to seekers and doubters. Such a personality which is in every way free and exemplary can transmit inner strength to many. But the pastor, instead of being occupied in pastoral care, is mainly caught up in services of baptism, confirmation, marriage and burial, and his ministry has assumed the character of that of an official for church affairs. At least these tasks take up so much of his time that the majority of the population come into contact with him only on such occasions.

'The pastor has become a poor, worried, bothered man who, like the rest of us, is subject to the modern style of life; who, like all of us, gets worked up by the times we live in, and who no longer has the strength to enable him to give us quietness, peace or faith. He is beginning, too, to be overcome by our *Zeitgeist*: speed, rationalization, bureaucratization.'

The more the Sunday services and the pastoral office fail to live up to people's expectations about them and so lead to disappointment, the more the occasional services fit into the understanding of the Church as a non-temporal reality. The occasions of birth, death, growing up and getting married demand a particular ceremony which is regarded as the normal practice, unaffected by one's individual experience or the historical epoch. The desire to keep to the safe path by following these customs is so strong that here there is usually an end to criticism and dissatisfaction with the Church, and even a pressure to conform, to which people by and large accede. The wish to do only what has always been done, and an unwillingness to make the personal effort to choose other forms, are sufficient motives to induce a demand for the occasional services.

'Since the war baptism and confirmation have once again become the general custom among us; my children must not be outsiders here.'
'As far as confirmation is concerned, the child ought to grow up as is customary, and then later on decide for himself if he will stay in the Church or not.'
'I have my child baptized and confirmed, so as not to have missed anything which might be useful to him later on.'
'I think a real wedding must include a church ceremony with bridal gown and veil and a solemn atmosphere in the church, with a reception afterwards at home, just as it was for my mother and grandmother. That adds the finishing touch.'

In addition, however, at the turning points of life questions arise about the whys and wherefores of existence which, in daily life, have receded into the background. In the face of these open questions, the individual looks for some kind of insurance. The Church might have an answer to these otherwise insoluble riddles. At least the Church has much more significance here than when it gets involved in the clash of public opinion or gives judgment in matters of daily conduct. Even if people cannot at present make anything out of the answers which the Church gives, they would not like completely to exclude the possibility of one day making use of them. A situation can all too easily arise in which only the unchanging and simple answer of the Church remains valid.

> 'It is a comforting thought to see the church buildings. You know there is something there which you can hold on to if need be.'
> 'You should have your child baptized, because in this way you place it under the protection of the Almighty.'
> 'I don't worry too much about Christian beliefs, but there must be baptism, confirmation, church marriages and church burials, for if I do not observe these ceremonies I have disregarded God, if he exists.'

(e) *Attitudes are interchangeable*

In general there are two themes which govern attitudes to the Church. The first runs: 'The Church must be more up to date. As a large organization covering the whole of society, it should be more powerful, more cohesive and more impressive, and must show more independent responsibility'. The second theme runs: 'The Church must have greater authenticity. In fitting its preaching to the needs of the small circle of the congregation and adopting a bureaucratic style, it risks becoming less authentic. The Church must understand that people regard it as being competent in the big questions of life which emerge from the background.' Both subjects are discussed with interest and passion, even when people are not personally involved and the conversation is merely an exchange of views about the Church. In such discussions there is always, to begin with, a preponderant tendency to criticize the Church and reprove it for not being up to date. The presence of these two attitudes is, however, of lesser significance than a further fact which throws real light on discussions about the Church. In conversation the participants jump, one might almost say methodically, from the one idea, that the Church must be more efficient and up to date, to the other, that the Church must be more itself. The person who criticizes the backwardness of the Church can at the same time emphasize its particularity and timelessness as an institution, and the person who emphasizes its special commission can immediately afterwards demand greater modernity from the Church. Both arguments are exchangeable for the individual, and may be put forward by the same person according to the circumstances of the conversation. They do not imply two hard and fast points of view held by different sections of the population, so much as two stereotyped ways of talking about the Church without allowing one's own convictions to intervene.

Group interview with several participants

> A: 'Every business man today knows that for long-term business affairs personal contacts must be cultivated over a period of years. Why does the Church not do this? Why does it think it can just work through the printed word? Why does it think it doesn't need to cultivate personal contacts?'
>
> B: 'Yes, of course that is necessary, but the parish areas are ridiculously large.'
>
> A: 'But you don't even have to make the contacts, they can be established in the service if you talk about ordinary daily concerns.'
>
> C: 'The Roman Catholic Church does much more to win people over. It fights for each soul. They even come into Protestant parishes. It is a question of organization.'
>
> A: 'But the Church isn't meant to be an organization.'
>
> *Interviewer:* 'Imagine for a moment that you were approached more often than up to now by the Church. Would that be right?'
>
> *All:* 'Yes, yes.'
>
> A: 'But that would in the long run only arouse interest if the pastor really had something to give one. So it's always a question of the personality of the pastor.'
>
> B: 'But that doesn't matter, for he represents the Church.'
>
> A: 'Yes, he represents the Church, but why is the Church not in a position to find and to train its people, so that they are able through the proclamation of God's Word to help people with their daily problems, so that they are modern, move with the times, and don't talk big words about the love of God—yes, that of course—but not only that? Why don't they create links with the Church from the sort of thoughts people think today? Too little is done in that way.'

(f) *Detachment through discussion*

Both these ideas about the Church stimulate the discussion about Christianity in general, and are an unfailing source of new material. The conversations lead to an impasse only when the individual is questioned directly about his attitude to Biblical proclamation, confession of faith, the Bible or the liturgy. Then it becomes clear that by and large people lack the knowledge to carry on a conversation on these subjects. They feel that they are knowledgeable about the Church, but there is a general uncertainty about assertions of faith, their content and meaning. Hence there arises the typical situation where discussion about proclamation and the contents of the faith is usually diverted into a discussion about the Church. People avoid questions about belief by discussing their social environment, and the place taken by the Church in it.

To change the subject in this way would not be critical, were it not that people approach even the terms of Biblical proclamation only in their connection with the Church. They can no longer hear these terms in their general sense; God is the God the Church talks about, the Ten

Commandments summarize the morals for which the Church is responsible, guilt is the guilt which the Church has loaded on itself by its failure, conviction and hope are the consolation which the Church and its members perhaps possess. With this approach, the individual stands outside as an observer, and by referring the discussion to the Church he evades the much more important questions about faith. Until the Church is more modern or more authentic, there is no point in knowing anything more about belief. As long as the Church is thus weak as a social organization and makes so feeble a stand itself for the central Christian assertions, faith cannot be much help. The image and conceptions of the Church block any further confrontation with the content of proclamation.

If discussion about the Church and knowledge about the content of belief tend to follow diverging courses, this is partly due to certain tendencies in public life today. Opinions about social institutions are much more widespread than actual confrontation with their activity and methods of work. The press, radio, television, literature and films give the individual an impression of what is going on, without his being personally involved or having to reach an assessment of them for his own sake. The level of information provided about public institutions is relatively high, but actual experience of the problems with which they are concerned does not keep pace with it.

Public information about questions of belief is traditionally given through instruction in school and confirmation classes, through sermons and Christian literature. However, a second, parallel channel of information about Christianity has for some time been gaining importance in the mass media which regularly reach a much wider public. In contrast to the specialist information about faith conveyed through teaching, preaching and Christian literature, the information given through the means of mass communication relates more with the social, political and moral aspects of the Church and its activity in society. Emphasis is given to the way the Church helps with life's problems, to its service to society and new developments in its work. Discussion about the Church is largely an exchange of views which have been stimulated by this second broad channel of information, or are a reaction to it. Any attempt to converse with people today about faith must reckon with the fact that the influence of information provided in the mass media about the Church far surpasses the effect of what is done to proclaim the Gospel through teaching, preaching and Christian literature. That place in the consciousness which was previously occupied by certain basic accepted beliefs, whether taken for granted or held with conviction, is now occupied by critical opinions about the Church and what it should or should not do.

Today proclamation of the Gospel itself can hardly alter or influence opinions about the Church, because one is faced with preconceptions which are already established before there is any contact with the local church or the Church's word. The attempt to let the actual situation in the local church speak for itself and by this to overcome preconceptions is ineffective. There is some recognition that the Church is different from what it seems to be, but this cannot do anything to alter the extremes of criticism which shape the image of the Church: 'If the Church is up to date, it should restrict itself to the timeless truths', or 'If it preaches the Gospel in the traditional way, it ought to be more contemporary'. Nor is it any use to challenge the correctness of these general opinions because they do not touch the nature and task of the Church. Conversation with friends, acquaintances or colleagues convinces the individual over and over again of the weight and social importance of the general arguments, and he finds these opinions about the Church confirmed on all sides. Any discussion which is concerned with the Church and attempts at this level to help one to reach clarification and a new understanding will not demolish prejudices; despite the good intention, it will only confirm preconceived ideas and enhance their social significance. As far as the vast majority of the general public is concerned, no new meeting with faith is possible through clarification of a person's relation to the Church and to its mission in the world.

3. THE ISSUE OF FAITH

(a) *The desire to believe*

Theologically speaking, one cannot separate the question of faith from that of the Church. The individual receives his profession of Christianity through the Church, and he retains this as a profession of faith in Jesus Christ only if he knows himself to be incorporated in the community of believers. But just as an individual in one particular situation does not find all the articles of the creed equally relevant or important, so too his relationship to the Church and congregation varies according to circumstances. In an extreme case, the external circumstances can even lead to a situation where, although he is indeed positively expecting to receive something from belief, the individual nevertheless sees no point in identifying himself on that account with the congregation and the Church in the form in which they now exist. Such an extreme attitude, where faith and the Church as an institution are seen as two different things, creates the incentive among the general public to become concerned with questions of faith. Independent of dogmatic formulations and specific creedal statements, people have an incipient desire to be able to believe. The desire is latent, and has its roots largely in the unconscious and the emotions; yet people are looking for certainty.

'One would like to believe, and through believing find security...'

People find themselves confronted with a wide variety of problems which cannot easily be solved by tackling them directly. These questions will never be answered through a few simple arguments, nevertheless one needs to be able to classify them in a certain order. It is hoped that faith will produce this order and insight. Behind the recognition that one's life lacks something of meaningfulness may lie hidden the straightforward search for truth.

There is evidence of considerable uneasiness about the need really to work something out in order to achieve true certainty and security. Here is a question which remains open and unanswered—a question one cannot get rid of, but can only push to one side in postponement. People do not come to terms with this open question by facing it consciously and then either accepting or rejecting it; rather they try, if possible, to suppress it. That the suppression is only superficial and temporary was revealed by the reactions of the respondents to the formal interrogation. For it was especially those who had a very distant relationship to their local church who took up an attitude of personal involvement towards the statements which far exceeded in sympathy that normally adopted towards an interesting subject. The alternative statements about faith provided in the interview brought to the surface of consciousness the type of questions which people usually simply put on one side. The statements suddenly gave these people the chance to struggle to reach definite convictions. The fact of discussing, in relatively plain and mutually contrasting statements, subjects such as the transitoriness of life, death, the meaning of life, belief, and the Church, awoke strong emotions.

> 'It's terrible, it gets under your skin, it has never been made so clear to me as here. In confirmation classes one was too young. It was like it was in school, you made jokes about the pastor and you were glad when you were outside again.'
> 'It makes me quite uncertain . . .'
> 'It worries me . . .'
> 'It disturbs me . . .'
> 'For years I haven't concerned myself with it to such an extent.'

To the desire to find security through believing there is a corresponding feeling of uncertainty about life and a vague fear. Although in today's society one is normally supposed to be self-confident and to enjoy decision-making, many people are prepared to admit this anxiety to themselves; this does not, however, mean that the Church and the Christian faith acquire any greater significance for them. The source of this dull sense of anxiety resides on the one hand in the idea that one can neither understand nor alter nor influence economic and political events in today's world. In the face of the incomprehensible trends and cross-relationships of a developed industrial society, one adopts an attitude of resignation or simply trusts to one's luck.

> 'You cannot any longer take in all the interconnected things which impinge on you.'
> 'Just read the paper; do you understand any more what is going on and why?'
> 'Who knows all the things that can happen to me if the ones up there wish it?'
> 'Things can't so easily go wrong with me. I trust to my luck.'
> 'Living in today's world, one often has a feeling of gloomy fear.'

The other source of insecurity is revealed when the question of the meaning of personal existence arises. Naturally for individuals the various goals of one's existence, ranging from the family to advancement in one's career and the enjoyment of one's declining years, play an important part. But in particular situations of stress—such as those created, for example, by an accident that makes it impossible to continue in one's accustomed occupation, or in critical experiences such as human failure, separation, and sudden death in the family or amongst one's friends—the question of the meaning of life is a more serious concern. These situations suggest the thought, 'This has happened to you, though you never imagined it could', or 'This has happened to someone else, and it could happen to you too at any time'. The consequences which individuals draw from such situations lead either to a superficial dismissal of the experience or a temporary feeling of assurance through the making of a good resolution. Nevertheless such reactions do not abolish the events, and some uncertainty remains. It is usually the case that thinking and reflection are no help in this kind of uncertainty, because ultimately one can know nothing of the purpose of existence.

'Sometimes everything seems senseless to me; then you ask yourself what purpose life really has.'
'Thinking about it doesn't get you anywhere; you soon reach the point where you don't know any more anyway, and you would rather give up thinking.'
'Sometimes life is like this, sometimes like that. Nothing lasts; what is fine passes more quickly than what is sad. Everyone comes one day to death's door. The important thing is to live for the day and to be able really to say, "Life is fine".'
'Sometimes I am afraid of the future.'

(b) *The primacy of intellectual proof*

Latent expectations regarding faith today are clearly very circumscribed. Men do not experience belief as a spontaneous and naïve process; rather, to believe means to be rationally convinced of something. Belief is subject to the primacy of intellectual proof. Because faith can really only be imagined as 'knowledgeable faith', people are largely unable (in contrast to what has already been said) to make anything of the contents of faith with which they may still be acquainted. The general feeling is, 'In the Church you can't look for or find knowledge'. Because of this demand for proof, the concept of 'to believe' has even changed its meaning in common parlance. It designates the hope that there is some probability of something desired taking place. Reliance is placed in the probability. In this sense the individual is more inclined to subscribe to scientific-positivist thought-forms, and to 'believe' rather that man can reach the planets, reform society and remove the last veil from the secrets of creation and life, than that God is merciful or that Jesus Christ is the Son of God.

'You can believe something or believe in something, if it is proved or there is a likely chance of its being proved.'

'I only believe what can be seen and can be proved precisely.'

Group interview with several participants:

Interviewer: 'Do you believe in God?'

A: 'You cannot prove his existence. Jesus Christ has been proved. Whether he is God's Son I doubt, even if he said so himself. Perhaps that was just a whim of his. I only believe that in his day he was the first person to preach humanity. And so in any case he was a great personality.'

B: 'I believe that as far as preaching humanity is concerned, there are others who have done that. All the great people of the past . . . But when Christ says he is God's Son, and you think that's a "whim", then for you the rest is equally unproven.'

A: 'Of course I could respect the man, the man and his wisdom and what he taught.'

B: 'But if he is crazy in one point, you cannot tell if the rest is true. God . . .'

A: 'Yes, God, you cannot prove that; of course that's something absolutely supernatural, whereas he was a man of flesh and blood. I cannot believe in God for this particular reason: if the story of creation is true—and I accept it as true—where does God come from? In any case the beginning of life is shrouded in darkness, and this is something which we shall never be able to work out with our own reasoning powers.'

C: 'I do not believe in God, but I do believe that there is a higher power. There must be some kind of institution which made everything.'

A: 'And where does it come from, this institution which made it?'

C: 'We cannot know that.'

A: 'I can only believe in something which can be proved. But I suppose that is no longer faith.'

A person's rational tendency causes him constantly to make use of scientific probability to oppose belief. But his self-confidence in doing so has in these days been fairly well shattered. Even the rejection of the Christian faith on the grounds of scientific proof has become a vague affair. Fifty years ago most people could give an account of Darwin's, Nietzsche's and Marx's thoughts and make them a basis for an atheistic position. With modern philosophy such a procedure is much harder, and as far as the discoveries of modern natural science are concerned, it is already impossible. Scientific thought is now no longer understood by the general public. It is much more a case of the people finding themselves obliged to accept the results of science because they see them applied around them all the time, though they can no longer follow the process by which the results are reached. It is becoming less and less possible to make use of scientific knowledge to 'disprove' faith. Yet their understanding of the problems is still inadequate to enable people to penetrate beyond scientific ways of thinking and to reach an understanding of the special function of belief.

(c) *Psychic release mechanisms*

A strong tension develops between the largely unconscious desire for safety and order which aims at gaining security in belief, and the insistence on rational proof under which the individual shelters. These two tendencies, the one a need for faith and the other an inability to believe (in the spontaneous-naïve sense), produce, from the psychological point of view, a strongly ambivalent attitude. The desire for order in questions about life is in conflict with the discredit which the intellect casts on faith. This contradiction is the signal for clearly defined psychic mechanisms by which the individual endeavours to escape quickly from the tension.

There are certain opinions which are taken as generally correct, being imposed by reason, and with these rationalizations the individual believes that he has settled the problem. He releases himself from questions of faith by appealing to moral conduct or criticizing the Church as an institution.

'I am a good living man, do no one any harm, then nothing can happen to me. I don't know if I believe in the resurrection and eternal life. But if I behave in a Christian way [i.e. morally], I shall be able to stand before my God at the last judgment, if there is a last judgment.'

'Believing may be a good thing, but the Church and the clergy are no good.'

People readily accept common prejudices about belief.

'Belief is out of date and unnecessary. The main thing is, you can rely on yourself.'

'One can only honour the inscrutable in silence.'

Furthermore, the tension between the search for security in faith and verification by the intellect induces a tendency to reduce the Christian faith to a private religion, or even to experiment with other possibilities of belief in the hope that they will fit in better with one's own views. Into this private religion the individual brings all the ideas which he can believe without difficulty, whilst excluding all the points or ideas which are disturbing or which could endanger the certainty of his convictions. Those who experiment with new beliefs turn mostly to philosophical theism, anthroposophy, and sectarian and Marxist theories.

The tendency to construct one's own belief in accordance with the measure of what one can believe can be illustrated by the following scale of opinions about the person of Jesus Christ. This is of course only an attempt to systematize the various attitudes adopted by the respondents in the enquiry, an attempt, however, which clearly reveals the presence of many different interpretations.

Jesus Christ is the Son of God, without any reservations.

Jesus Christ is a man, a person who made history, a fanatical believer, a martyr.

Jesus Christ is a symbol of man. He has no historical existence. In him are united the perfection and eternity of the divine part in man and the imperfection and finiteness of human existence. In Jesus these two forces are revealed in their absolute inseparability and tragedy.

Jesus Christ is the image for man in his struggle with his God.

Jesus Christ's life and suffering describe symbolically the way man must take in order to reach God.

Jesus Christ is the prototype and the example of good and of willingness to believe.

The justification for speaking of psychic mechanisms of release and of a reduction of belief to a private religion is deduced from the fact that the individual solves questions of belief without himself understanding very much about the assertions he is making. The chief characteristic of the situation is that an attitude for or against faith is adopted on the basis of extremely little knowledge. The extent of knowledge is only such as a person might retain from confirmation classes attended without much application some twenty years ago, at the age of 13 or 14. It is, therefore, hard to relate such use of rationalizing arguments to the conflict between reason and revelation in the contemporary world. The fact that people make generalizations and reduce faith to those opinions they can personally uphold does not mean that they definitely object to the 'folly' of the Gospel or the fact that it cannot be rationally substantiated. Rationalization may seem to lead to a clear and unambiguous attitude, but it evades a real intellectual confrontation with the content of belief. If such a confrontation does happen, people feel immediately that they must try to work out a personal re-evaluation of the problem, guided by reason. In a similar way, private religion thrives on the failure to perceive the difference between faith and knowledge. It is only those people who do not realize that faith is something which leads them beyond their own opinions, and summons them to wider obligations, who succeed in reducing the contents of faith to what they themselves are capable of believing. The fact that they are intent on the quest for superficial, rational certainty actually prevents them from finding that security in firm conviction for which emotionally they are striving. In any case, knowledge of the contents of the faith would surely be of help in the demand for rational insight, as well as the desire for firm conviction, regardless of whether the provision of better information leads to a more firmly based and more certain acceptance of faith or to a denial of it.

(d) *Reasons for lack of knowledge about the faith*

Rationalization and the attempt to construct a private system of belief do little to resolve the tension between the desire for faith and the demand for intellectual proof. Therefore the further question arises as to what is the reason for the poor standard of knowledge of the faith. The discussion in which biblical proclamation takes place within the local church is very different from the general discussion in which the vast mass of church members are involved through their private lives and interests. In a local church, discussion about faith and the answers given concerning it have become a debate internal to the institution. The person who knows very well that he does not measure up to the Church's expectations in conduct and knowledge, regards himself as automatically excluded from the discussion and is forced to the conclusion that the exchange of views in the local church takes place at a level which is much too elevated and specialist for him. The questions which he would want to put are not such as would be discussed between convinced Christians. It is not that the information conveyed in the local church's preaching is dismissed as inappropriate, but rather that, in the opinion of the general public, it is directed at people who with great piety have already made a firm decision.

'Protestant faith is a religion for those who are already firm and strong in matters of faith.'

'Of course through your baptism you are vaguely involved, but you still feel you don't really belong. When you meet believers, you always feel an outsider.'

Before a person can concern himself with the information imparted by preaching, he must, socially speaking, make a decision. The individual is obliged to take personal steps to establish a relationship with the local church and to identify himself with it. This situation is reflected in the normal understanding of Christians as not primarily people who know their faith, but as those who have made a 'decision'. The average church member, however, regards himself at most as one who is still looking for the way; he wants to understand something, and still has to make up his mind. In surmounting this hurdle of coming to a definite decision, such a person receives no support from having a connection with like-thinking people and through an exchange of views with them. The individual does not even know what he is letting himself in for if he makes such a decision, nor how he can justify it, for, apart from the information to be gained from the local church, everyone else who surrounds him shares his own uncertainty and ignorance in matters of belief.

'In one's seeking and decision-making one is left to oneself and gets no help.'

'At a time when no one can find his way without reacting to the ideas of others, and can make a terrible mistake if he does not, he has to rely entirely on himself.'

'In questions of belief you flounder; there is nothing to hold on to, and no clear requirement. I feel I am not adequately informed in matters of belief to be able to make the right decision.'

The prominence which decision has in the matter of being a Christian also explains the usual attitude of parents with regard to the religious upbringing of their children. Because they themselves are not 'convinced' or 'decided' Christians, and feel themselves inadequately informed, they hand over the task of religious education to external institutions, the school and the local church. The child himself must later make his own decision about being a Christian.

'My children were baptized; they must have religious instruction and be confirmed like the others, and then they must make up their own minds what they want.'

If biblical proclamation in the local church cannot be regarded as a source of information because it is tied up with the particular situation of the convinced Christians, the vast majority of the population finds itself also unable to gather information about faith in other ways outside the local church. It is the general opinion that there is really no point in going into the content of faith on one's own account, because one would never be able to reach an understanding of it.

'Without the right explanations you cannot really understand the Bible. You can see this from the fact that it is interpreted in such different ways. Protestant and Catholic Christians, the Orthodox and all the sects, Jehovah's Witnesses, Adventists, Baptists, Mormons and the rest of them, they all base their beliefs on this one book; yet they all think different things and all say that they alone are right and the others are all heretics.'

'You cannot simply believe literally in all that is in the Bible, like our grandparents and great-grandparents did. And when you hear from the children what they are told in religious education at school, it is just the same as we had it. And even then we were suspicious of it and regarded it more as fairy tales. What can one say in answer to their critical questions?'

The disillusionment here expressed has its foundation in the fact that exposition is lacking. People accept the assertions of the faith as general truths, but are then unable to connect them with their own situation. There is no wrestling with the Christian truths on the basis of convictions already held. Because the 'point' of the assertions of the faith and their relation to the individual are not clear, there is no use in trying on one's own to find out more about them. The occasional church-goer, when he does attend church, expresses his disappointment thus:

'It's always the same, what they produce. What use is faith to me?'
'What help is the preaching of faith to me?'
'Every time I come out of church I ask myself, What did I get out of it? What can I make of the sermon? What then has faith to offer me?'

(e) *Change in the way knowledge is appropriated*

The lack of basic information about faith should be seen against the following background. In order to be up to date in public affairs today, knowledge about the Church, but not about belief, is required and people find no link between general Christian truths and their own personal existence. One is prompted to examine carefully the problem of the level of information, but not by the complaints of theologians about people's ignorance. These have often been heard and the theologians have sometimes used very approximate standards to assess the state of knowledge. There has, however, been a change in the way one 'learns' in the realm of convictions and beliefs. The incentive to consider the contents of the faith increases when these are subjects of public interest and one can participate responsibly in their discussion. Previously the assertions of faith were subjects of public interest, in that people of authority in local politics expressed their views about them, and the example of these men provided the opportunity to agree or disagree. Through certain personalities in local society, Christian views gained the interest of the community, and they were also lived out concretely in the presence of others.

> 'I grew up in the country, and we had a pastor who was accepted and respected by the whole village, even the worst-living farmers. He spoke "*platt Deutsch*" dialect, was happily married, knew a bit about agriculture, hadn't studied too much, but was on the best of terms with the good Lord, and could show us that too. For everyone in every situation he had the right word and the right comfort. His sermons were understood; now and again he could let out a "*Donnerwetter*". He visited his parishioners constantly in their homes. He was a man who brought Christianity near to you and preserved it for you.'

Furthermore, knowledge of the faith was included in the education given at home. In order to have an independent and personal opinion in public affairs and to enable one to bring common human ideals to bear in such affairs, an acquaintance with the contents of the faith was regarded as essential. Since this education was carried out in the family at home, with a view to its use later in life, the convictions there acquired were also linked from the beginning with actual persons and experiences.

> 'I grew up in a home where both parents were very highly educated. My father was a high-school teacher, my mother was very artistic, and both my parents were genuinely and naturally devout. In the evenings mother used often to tell me very graphically stories from the life of Jesus. As a child I used to share in the experience of the biblical events, in their joy and in their suffering. I simply grew up into them. For me there is no doubt, and I find it terrible to see people today living out their lives pointlessly and aimlessly . . .'

Within today's widely extended society, which is structured by the aims of the various organizations, public attention depends increasingly upon the mass media. Neither the local community nor the common concerns of private individuals can today produce themes of general moment. Listening to sermons and attending religious instruction are more and more becoming a special behaviour through which the individual links himself with a particular social group. It is only through the means of mass communication that one can establish a broad general level of information and a certain degree of knowledge which could give men once more the freedom to decide in their wavering between the desire for security in belief and the demand for intellectual proof. Discussions about the church, and similarly about other social organizations, show that these means of communication are certainly able to instil general knowledge into the community at large.

(f) *Providing information about faith instead of presenting a modernized Church appearance*

The extent to which information conveyed by mass media can establish a link with personal situations and thus make clear the 'point' of believing depends today on two conditions. The Church must be prepared to follow a different course from that of the economic, political and cultural organizations in society. These are competing in the field of public opinion mainly for tacit and automatic recognition, and their real activities remain more or less hidden from the public eye, because of the very specialized concerns which are involved. In contrast the Church, instead of concentrating on making known to the public the political, diaconal or cultural aspects of its life, must openly display the very focal point of its involvement. Of course a careful understanding of the faith also requires some theology, and theological ways of thinking are implied into which an individual must slowly grow. But any information about faith which has an institutional slant or concentrates on the Church as a social organization would, in view of the existing detachment from and criticism of the Church, merely give the impression of an ecclesiastical publicity campaign. Such information would again only serve to promote general discussion about the Church, and not about faith.

The information provided should in addition contain as much interpretation as possible, and at the same time emphasize only the basic data necessary for Christian faith. Interpretation is essential if the recipient is really to come to grips with the articles of faith. If the information emphasizes the basic data for faith, there is no possibility of avoiding the essential point. When under emotional or intellectual tension, people are particularly sensitive in their reaction to an exposition which avoids the actual problem as they feel it, probably for the very reason that skirting around questions of belief is so widely and commonly practised. In these circumstances, practically speaking, the way is open for an interpretation of the biblical story by means of modern drama and visual aids, and this does not at all mean restricting oneself to a purely historical portrayal. The Old and New Testaments are not the Church, but within them are found the basis both for the Church and for faith; and people know this. The themes of the biblical narrative also prevent the exposition from becoming flat, because they are told briefly. Nevertheless they are capable of dramatic adaptation, to form an event which will grip the interest of the listener or viewer.

In order to lead general discussion about the Church on to the much more important debate about faith, the Church must ask how far it may be able to use mass communication to put over effective information about faith. Here lies the decisive opportunity to help the vast majority of church members, who want to believe and find security in belief and yet are perplexed by intellectual doubts, to find clarity. One should, however, entertain no illusions in this matter. A careful attempt of this kind in itself bears no guarantee of automatic success for the Church. The resistance which the information will meet and which it will stimulate comes from a wholesale positivist criticism of religion and of intellectual ways of thought which have an idealistic origin.

7

'A man who thinks in progressive terms cannot believe in a God of ideas, in a God who is only a working hypothesis. Modern man creates the world formula and knowledge is his faith.'

'It is my opinion that the whole Christian faith is aimed at keeping men dumb. Religion is the opium of the masses, that is still my opinion today, and I will not depart from that opinion.'

'I believe only in the triumph of the human spirit, and not in God.'

'Christendom should have arisen in Rome or Athens, for then it would have had maturity and intrinsic coherence for a thinking person. In its present form it is not acceptable to a thinking person. It is a religion of the east, and will always remain so.'

Any attempt to reveal the central concern of the Church and to provide information about it necessarily involves the risk of producing a more definite rejection. For this reason the venture cannot be understood as aiming at a superficial type of publicity. Its decisive importance resides in the fact that it should offer the individual church member above all the equipment necessary for him to acquire an attitude to the Church and congregation which is formed on better foundations.

4. NON-CHRISTIAN RELIGIOSITY?

(a) *From analysis of opinions to research into motivations*

How does the contemporary church member experience the faith? An attempt has been made to answer this question in the preceding findings through an analysis of straightforward reactions and replies to the theme. The individual stated his views for or against the Church and for or against faith, and gave the reasons that led him to this position. But it is obvious that his attitude is also shaped by motivations which, as far as his judgment and understanding are concerned, have nothing to do with the subject of faith. Such basic motivations are too general to be reflected directly in discussion about the tasks of the Church and the content of faith. Though the respondent cannot verbalize these influences, they nevertheless strongly influence his behaviour and convictions. Because they are rooted also in other realms of life, they have a much more decisive effect on his behaviour and convictions than this or that particular reaction to the claims of the Church or to a statement of Christian faith.

However, not only do the respondents limit their replies according to their own ideas as to what is essential and non-essential for the subject, but their interpretations of events around the Church also often follow a very simplified model. They contrast a 'traditional' understanding of faith with a 'modern' or 'contemporary' understanding. They talk about a 'distant' or a 'close' relationship to the Church. These models describe more than the mere acceptance or rejection of the Christian message. They connect Christian conviction with a general outlook upon life. Faith is sometimes apprehended through a basic conception inherited from the past, and at others it is associated with an outlook which is open to the present; it is sometimes linked with a basically individualistic attitude, but at others it is conditioned by an attitude which on the whole is open to community interests. In the case of such interpretations, however, it is not at all clear whether it is really an adequate description of the situation to assume that there are two opposed basic attitudes.

The 111 statements for or against the faith presented to the church members in the formal interrogation widened the range of replies beyond popular arguments and limited knowledge in matters of faith. The variety of assertions enabled the informants to project their motivations into the responses. Although the statements had the function of directing people to the essential issues, they remained of course bound to the beliefs which the church members themselves felt to be important and controversial.

The instrument of factor analysis, applied to the graded material drawn from the formal interrogation, rendered it possible to reach clearer distinctions in the basic motivations concerning belief. (Among the whole range of reactions, factor analysis highlights common determinants.) It selects from the total number of answers of all the respondents those which to a high degree of probability seem to be expressed by all and held in common. (cf. Appendix 1: Explanation of the Methods Employed.) Groups of related reactions are compiled which clearly differ from other groupings, and point to a more general motivation or a determining 'factor' behind the individual answers. Thus in the following lists of statements which make up a factor, each assent or denial refers to the same attitude. The analysis produces only as many groupings and underlying motivations as are necessary to classify the complete field of choices. Therefore, beyond the limited number of motivations, no other basic influences are at work in regard to the issues covered by the statements.

The basic motivations are independent of and distinct from one another. But there are also connections between them. Some motivations go closely together, whereas others are at almost opposite poles. Furthermore, one finds replies and reactions which give equal support to two different motivations and are meaningful for both of them. These interrelations point to transitions between the basic influences, and show reciprocal dependencies among the motivations. Those decisions in particular which lie at the meeting points between the general socio-psychological factors are most revealing for the perspective of faith. They indicate conflicting areas in which the church members in particular get to grips with Christian challenges. Hence in the following sections the number of basic motivations in the field of belief are first surveyed. It is then possible, using a more structural interpretation, to deal with the question whether or not answers to life's problems which are no longer Christian are spreading in the behaviour pattern of general Christianity.

(b) *Basic motivations in the field of belief*

The results of the formal interviews reveal a complex but limited picture of the motivations which are at work today in the field of belief.

It seems complex if one supposes that today faith and unbelief create decisive and unequivocal attitudes which can be judged by church attendance or agreement with the articles of faith. The picture seems astonishingly limited if one reflects on the number of far-reaching and difficult questions dealt with in the statements, such as the meaning of personal existence, the transitoriness of life situations, fear of the future, the threat of death, love of one's neighbour, faith in God and Jesus Christ, the evaluation of the Church's occasional services. (Cf. Appendix 2: Table of Statements.) There is the additional fact that the respondents came from all social classes in the population and were identified with the Church in different degrees. (Cf. Appendix 3, and p. 67.)

The basic motivations each point in a particular direction, but they can coalesce in an individual or in a group of those questioned. They characterize, not individual persons or groupings, but the forces which are determinate in the inner debate about faith. There are altogether six basic motivations which comprehend the total accounting of church members for the subjects treated in the statements. There are no further differentiations in basic motives.

1. Intellectualization: Questions about the meaning and purpose of life are overcome by rational arguments.
2. General fear: Insecurity of not knowing what faces one in the future or in one's social environment.
3. Identification restricted to experiences around one's own person: Interest in the immediate circumstances around one's own person, and inability to feel secure in wider spheres of existence.
4. Opportunism: Superficial adoption of the given conditions, without any point of view of one's own.
5. Self-centred materialism: Lack of trust and lack of openness towards others and towards more comprehensive convictions.
6. Attitude of faith: Confirming the essential statements of Christian faith.

(c) *Intellectualization*

The most common disposition amongst church members is that of intellectualization. Their recourse to arguments and rational considerations reveals the widespread feeling that something needs to be mastered or worked out. Facing the questions of purpose in life, most people are no longer satisfied with unreflective modes of conduct, but need a certain rational orientation that will justify their behaviour or provide a foundation for it.

The following statements define this compulsion towards intellectualization:

124. The meaning of life consists in acquiring the best possible and most extensive education. (70)
123. The meaning of life consists in acquiring the widest possible knowledge. (65)
122. The meaning of life consists in getting on in one's occupation. (46)

125. The meaning of life consists in doing something which is valuable, not only for myself, but also for other people. (43)
92. Man today is on intimate terms with death. Death has lost its power to terrify the individual. (42)
95. The thought of death compels me to live my life so that, when I die, everything will be in order. (40)
101. Unless you continually consider the transitoriness of the moment, you cannot lead a reasonable life. (35)
119. The meaning of life consists in doing one's best to lead a morally irreproachable life. (33)

In the table above and in the following tables, the numbers in front of the statements indicate their place in the complete list in Appendix 2. The figures in brackets after the statements indicate how strong a constituent the statement is in this motivation. The ratings are defined by comparing the replies of all informants with the total number of statements. The consistency of a reaction is measured in the context of each reply to each statement of each informant. The importance of a statement for the motivation rises in a scale of 1 to 100 in the affirmative, and in a scale of −1 to −100 in negations.

People find general answers to the questions about the meaning of life in their education, knowledge, work and altruism. The mention of these ideals does not, of course, say anything about the extent to which they are regarded as really serious and binding. The choices are rather evidence that the individual has been compelled to give some thought to the matter and engage in reflection. At this general level, it is still undecided by what inner attitudes these deliberations are fed or to what attitudes they will lead. Only one result is already very obvious. If one thinks about the whole of life, death is included in the consideration as an inevitable event. But because death is so automatically one of the considerations and can be grasped firmly, it poses no problems. There is not much mystery which could become a reason to ask deeper and religious questions. Death is not regarded as the decisive threat to life. It is, of course, a point of reference for the question about meaning in life, but it is not the first or the only one.

(d) *General fear, and identification restricted to experiences around one's own person*

The incentive for intellectualization has its origin in two fairly general psychological tendencies: a general fear, and an identification only with desires and anxieties in the sphere surrounding one's own person. Fear challenges one to reflect upon one's own situation and to bring forward various arguments. If people today concentrate only on their own small world, they wish to provide reasons for this one-sided interest. Insecurity, as well as the feeling that they have made a restriction in their lives, awakens their need for general orientation.

The widespread sense of uncertainty in face of the realities of personal existence and of the environment causes the main tendency in the motivation of general fear. This became evident even in the exploratory surveys.

The following statements define the motivation of general fear:

86. Sometimes I am afraid of death. (69)
83. Sometimes I am afraid of the future. (66)
85. Sometimes I am afraid of sickness. (63)
82. Living in today's world, one often has a feeling of gloomy fear. (61)
84. Sometimes I am afraid of growing old. (61)
110. I can best fight against fear by trying to forget it in work. (47)

Identification restricted to the world of experience immediate to oneself (with a lack of trust in wider spheres of life) is a motivation which has a greater influence on faith than any of the attitudes described hitherto. This tendency is paralleled by a detached attitude towards the inter-relationships and institutions of the social environment which govern one's life. Public programmes and measures calling for the responsible co-operation of the individual can also be carried out without much response from or participation by the people. Concentration on personal affairs has a much greater effect, however, upon faith as a conviction which interprets one's relationship to one's neighbour, to history and to the world. If all one's attention is concentrated on one's own small experiences, such a disposition must clash with that objectivity and all-embracing reality of which faith speaks. No public institution, however, can provide the individual with the answer to his search for all-embracing convictions that he can rely on. For this reason, in matters of faith a clear contrast emerges between the concern for wider realities, and dedication to one's self and experiences in the small sphere of personal life.

The following statements define the attitude of identification restricted to experiences around one's own person:

Assent:

71. I find confirmation of God's existence in the rule of nature, not in the Christian faith. (53)
102. If I had always to think about the transitoriness of the moment, I should lose all joy in life. (45)
3. I do not worry about the hereafter; I just do my best to do my duty in my occupation and towards my family. (42)
112. I can best fight against fear by trusting to my strength, my ability and my luck. (39)
99. The thought of the end of my life makes me so afraid that I put it well on one side. (38)
76. Sometimes I have the feeling that I am powerless in the hand of fate, and that even God cannot help. (36)
1. I don't worry about what might happen after my death, but take each day as it comes. (34)
2. My motto is: 'Live your life to the full, for after death there is nothing'. (34)

Rejection:

118. I have no fear because I believe in the immortality of my
soul. (−48)
23. I would risk my own life for faith in Jesus Christ. (−40)
117. I have no fear because I trust in God. (−38)
35. The Christian faith gives me security at all times. (−34)
89. The thought of death does not terrify me, because I believe
in the immortality of the soul. (−32)
22. The well-being of the community to which I belong is of
more value to me than my own life. (−31)

The statements to which assent is given coalesce into one simple point of view. It can be summarized, 'I am concerned about what is immediate to myself'. A reality which could extend beyond the sphere of the present and the realm of family and work is consciously excluded. Instead, people care about their happiness and concentrate on their own luck and sometimes on their own helplessness. Spheres of existence which transcend the narrow realm of personal experience are increasingly rejected in the following order: the community, belief in God, the rule of Jesus Christ, and eternal life. This rejection is not based on the conviction that those more extensive relationships in which men could feel themselves at home do not exist. It is merely that for those who make an exclusive identification with experiences around their own person, such wider relationships make no contribution to their feeling safe and secure. Because those aspects of life which extend beyond the narrow sphere of existence are not considered, they also afford no support.

(e) *Opportunism and self-centred materialism*

To those very widespread basic attitudes already considered, two other motivations have to be added. These are opportunism, which reflects the significance of Christendom as a tradition in society, and self-centred materialism, which depends on early upbringing and the subsequent growth of personality.

In the case of opportunism, arguments about faith are overlaid by the problem of finding one's place in society. Because society is Christian and no other socially binding views are available, rejection of faith would involve the risk of isolating oneself and stepping out from generally accepted social patterns. The individual is not willing to run this risk. He is not willing lightly to throw away the advantage provided, psychologically speaking, by traditional conduct, because it relieves him of the need to give the matter any special thought or to decide what attitude to adopt. Although he cannot make much out of the contents of the faith, behind the Church and faith there may yet stand a greater authority than it is possible at the moment to recognize.

The following statements define the motivation of opportunism:

44. I don't worry much about Christian belief, but one must have baptism, confirmation, church weddings and church burials, because they are the accepted thing in our culture. (66)

45. I don't worry much about Christian belief, but one must have baptism, confirmation, church weddings and church burials, for if I do not observe these ceremonies, I have disregarded God, if He exists. (63)

55. I am a Christian, because this is natural according to tradition and custom. (55)

62. I believe in Jesus Christ, so that things may go well for me on earth. (54)

47. You should have your child baptized, so that it does not seem an outsider later on. (53)

41. I am glad I was baptized, because this means I can have a Christian burial. The idea of simply being put into the ground without a church ceremony is one I find unpleasant. (50)

6. Above all, one should behave in such a way that after death one is remembered with respect. (49)

The opportunistic attitude is maintained particularly with reference to the occasional services of baptism, confirmation, marriage and burial as fixed rites. They make up the socially obligatory character of Christianity. In comparison, personal conviction plays a subordinate role. It is rated as peripheral. There is, however, some recognition of the inconsequential nature of such an attitude. Associated with acceptance of the occasional services is a minimum of superficial consent to statements about the Christian faith such as 'God could exist as a source of authority', 'Belief in Jesus Christ could have some significance for one's good fortune'.

Characteristic of self-centred materialism is the self-confident attitude of being primarily concerned with one's own advantage and one's own precious life. Lack of trust in one's fellow-men and a lack of openness with regard to ideas which involve common commitment predominate. The relationship to one's fellow-men and the willingness to devote oneself to common interests of any kind are obstructed. Self-centred materialism denies that one needs the assistance or advice of others. If this denial is made without reflection, then this opinion is hardly the result of experiences and decisions which have consciously led to such a judgment. The attitude has rather its origin in early childhood and in the development of personality itself. The validity of the judgments expressed is never questioned. The problems are suppressed, in favour of a simplified way of thought in which the individual is so firmly rooted that no other opinions or doubts can reach him.

The motivation of self-centred materialism is defined by the following statements:

Assent:

77. I believe only in the triumph of the human spirit, and not in God. (59)
120. The meaning of life consists in having one day a lot of money. (58)
32. The Christian faith is nothing more than a help to make dying easier. (53)
34. The Christian faith is primarily something for the weak and helpless, children and old people. (49)
2. My motto is: 'Live your life to the full, for after death there is nothing'. (48)
75. I believe that it is men alone who by their work shape history, and not God. (46)
121. The meaning of life consists in having experienced and savoured the taste of everything to the full. (46)
51. I do not believe in the immortality of the soul, because death shows me that everything is transitory. (44)
73. God is only a construct of the mind made in the face of the finality and inevitability of death. (43)
15. I don't think much of loving your neighbour. My attitude is, 'If you want a thing done, you must do it yourself'. No one else will help me. (41)

Rejection:

58. I believe that Christ desires the true happiness of all men. (−47)
21. I would risk my life for the sake of my family. (−43)
17. How I am to God is shown in how I am to those people who are entrusted to me. (−41)
24. The man who has never learnt that human life acquires its value in devotion to others, does not know the true meaning of life. (−41)

Among the positive answers, the main ideas are having much money, experiencing and enjoying everything to the full, and emphasizing the autonomy of man. The attitude of self-centred materialism regards faith as a contrary position. To believe, in the way Christian doctrine understands it, is impossible because holding such convictions would mean retreating from one's own ways of thought. In the realm of those statements which are rejected, there is the aggravating factor that any kind of sacrifice or devotion is rated negatively. There is no experience of the fact that the individual must give out, or share himself with others, so as to get in return solidarity with his fellow-men or breadth of outlook. There is only a limited ability to open oneself, and this limitation even affects relations with the family and extends further to relations with one's neighbours and commitment to faith.

(f) *The attitude of faith*

Finally, the attitude of faith itself is to be considered. Among all the motivations, the attitude of faith is the most clearly accentuated. It takes the form of an assent to the essential content of faith. Since half of the respondents were church-goers attending church at least once a month, the attitude of faith is strongly represented.

The following statements define the attitude of faith:

Assent:

56. I believe in Jesus Christ, because in his actions and words God Himself acts and speaks. (85)
64. Jesus is the resurrection and the life; he who believes in him will live, even if he dies. And he who believes in him in this life will not die in eternity. (85)
63. Jesus is God's Son; he is the man for us all; he takes our place, for he died for us on the cross. (83)
57. I believe in the power of Christ to forgive me all my sins irrevocably. (82)
70. In Jesus Christ I find confirmation of the fact that God exists. (81)
7. I believe that God will judge me at the Last Day. (81)
12. Earthly life is only a stage on the way to eternal life. (81)
108. Christ is the risen one, who takes us up into his resurrection. All that we can do, and all the powers at our disposal, are pious self-deception in the face of the power of death. We can be liberated from death only by Jesus Christ. (81)
59. I believe that at the end of time Christ will restore justice and love to this whole torn world. (81)

Rejections:

68. Jesus is not the Son of God, but only a historical person. (−72)
25. You are on your own; the Christian faith is no help to anyone. (−71)

This attitude relies on confessional statements of faith. This raises the question whether the factor is concerned only with assent to formulated faith, or whether it is concerned also with real behaviour based on faith. The statements give no guide as to what the person experiences in regard to faith or with faith. It is not possible to define what function these statements have in the life of the individual. But on the other hand one cannot imagine any actual attitude of faith which is not pledged at least to a critical re-evaluation of the sentences and concepts contained in the statements. Assent to the statements, perhaps as a preliminary expression of one's own experience, and an express rejection of the negative opinions about the point of Christian faith and the person of Jesus Christ, must be rooted also in a practical relationship to faith. The factor is correlated to a high degree with regular church attendance. About 70% of the church-goers manifest this motivation. Hence one can say that the attitude of faith not only comprehends readiness to believe the confessional statements, but also includes actual behaviour based on faith.

(g) *Support for a non-Christian religiosity*

Among all the church members, the field of debate about belief is governed by various basic motivations which mark the different ways in which men approach ideas about faith. To this must be added the attitude of faith itself. In order to clarify the problem of non-Christian religiosity amongst church members, it is necessary to examine the attitude of faith in relation to the other tendencies. It is important to keep the following image in mind. When an individual concerns himself with finding an answer to questions about the meaning of life, its transitoriness, death, love of one's neighbour, the reality of God, Jesus Christ and the Church, his motivations pull him in various directions. The power of each motivation depends not least on the kind of allies and opponents which it has in the field. When the situation is understood in terms of forces and opposing forces reacting on each other, it is necessary to appreciate the interaction of these motivations and the distribution of the various trends. Any separation of the attitude of faith from all the other basic motivations, which with their affirmations lead in other directions, would be a significant sign of the emergence of a non-Christian religiosity within general Christianity. If the attitude of faith is supported by certain basic motivations and clearly denied by others, this contradiction would point to the fact that the population is strongly aware of a conflict in matters of faith.

(h) *Self-centred materialism opposed to the attitude of faith*

Among all the basic motivations, self-centred materialism, with its lack of trust and openness, forms the opposite pole to the attitude of faith. The lack of willingness to risk anything for other people or put any trust in fundamental convictions, can almost be called a complete inability to believe. Accordingly those statements which positively support the attitude of faith are clearly rejected, and those which represent a decisive denial of it are strongly affirmed.

Motivation 6: Attitude of Faith
Motivation 5: Self-centred Materialism

		6	5
56.	I believe in Jesus Christ, because in his actions and words God Himself acts and speaks.	+85	−12
58.	I believe that Christ desires the true happiness of all men.	+62	−47
17.	How I am to God is shown in how I am to those people who are entrusted to me.	+49	−41

	6	5
68. Jesus is not the Son of God, but only a historical person.	−72	+16
25. You are on your own; the Christian faith is no help to anyone.	−71	+29
75. I believe that it is men alone who by their work shape history, and not God.	−57	+46
2. My motto is: 'Live your life to the full, for after death there is nothing'.	−46	+48

In the comparison of the factors, the most important statements are those which contribute positively or negatively to both motivations in large degree. They show the relationship between the attitudes. The factors are above all independent of one another. Therefore the statements which support one factor to a high degree are irrelevant for the other factors.

The table above, and the following tables in which different factors are compared, give only a limited number of the most significant statements. Other statements fit into the same pattern. For a more detailed analysis, see the diagrams in Appendix 4.

(i) *Neutral motivations: General Fear and Opportunism*

The motivation of general fear and uncertainty stands in a neutral relationship to the polarity between the attitude of faith and self-centred materialism. The attitude of faith does not generally overcome this type of uncertainty, nor does general fear reinforce faith in such a way that people who are especially affected by this uncertainty find refuge and strength in faith.

Motivation 6: Attitude of Faith
Motivation 2: General Fear

	6	2
86. Sometimes I am afraid of death.	−1	+69
83. Sometimes I am afraid of the future.	−4	+66
85. Sometimes I am afraid of sickness.	−0	+83

Fear can be overcome in very different ways. There are a number of solutions to the problem of dispelling uncertainty. Amongst them trust in God, or the concern to be right with God, have the same importance as fatalism or simple resignation.

Motivation 6: Attitude of Faith.
Motivation 2: General Fear.

	6	2
97. The thought of death compels me to try some time or other to get right with God.	+55	−32
117. I have no fear because I trust in God.	+58	−33

76. Sometimes I have the feeling that I am powerless
in the hand of fate, and that even God cannot help.   −44   +44
 1. I don't worry about what might happen after my
death, but take each day as it comes.   −40   +34

The attitude of opportunism is also relatively independent of the tension between the attitude of faith and denial of Christian concepts. Since a utilitarian viewpoint predominates and a position either for or against belief is not taken up, a lack of clearly defined convictions is connected with this attitude. Opportunism reflects approximately the amount of Christianity which is regarded as necessary to keep up with the general patterns in society. This conventional Christianity is already very close to a rejection of the attitude of faith.

Motivation 6: Attitude of Faith.
Motivation 4: Opportunism.

		6	4
55.	I am a Christian, because this is natural according to tradition and custom.	−8	+55
44.	I don't worry much about Christian belief, but one must have baptism, confirmation, church weddings and church burials, because they are the accepted thing in our culture.	−19	+66
126.	The meaning of life consists in being able to say at the end of one's life, 'I have attained all I wanted'.	−35	+40
37.	Everything is laid down by fate, and in this even the Christian faith is no help.	−57	+36

In opportunism, however, a second element comes into play. It can best be understood as a desire for a security within the sphere of faith, free of the compulsion to reflect. It is a desire to live in a world of Christian ideas which is taken for granted, and thus free from any doubts and challenges.

Motivation 6: Attitude of Faith.
Motivation 4: Opportunism.

		6	4
45.	I don't worry much about Christian belief, but one must have baptism, confirmation, church weddings and church burials, for if I do not observe these ceremonies, I have disregarded God, if He exists.	+1	+63
62.	I believe in Jesus Christ, so that things may go well for me on earth.	+22	+53
61.	I believe in Jesus Christ, so that on the Last Day I may enter God's Kingdom.	+56	+35

(j) *Trend towards a non-Christian creed*

The first conclusion drawn from the discovery of a widespread intellectualization was that this was a formal development: the need for rational arguments about life. However, comparison with the motivation of self-centred materialism reveals that the rationalizing answers are largely following the line of criticism of faith and creed. Even on the subject of belief, most people today feel obliged to give priority to rational considerations. Fear and insecurity, as well as the feeling of restriction to the narrow sphere of one's own experiences, produce a need for a general orientation. And so when questions about the meaning of life and its broader concerns demand an answer, the opinions readily at hand to help provide it are increasingly those which, pressing the necessity of 'reasonable' argumentation, do away with faith. Rationalizing considerations help to sublimate and excuse a narrow self-centred attitude, by means of generally accepted views. There is an increasing tendency for generally valid insights to coincide in people's minds with an open rejection of faith.

Intellectualization serves only to a very much lesser extent to open men's consciences to their solidarity with their neighbours and to an overarching order in life. Then these rational considerations introduce from outside new points of view which influence the individual's own attitude. The use of the intellect here serves to awaken understanding of the necessity to devote oneself to a cause or to common endeavours, and in this way to achieve a widening of one's horizons. In such cases intellectualization conflicts with the attitude of self-centred materialism.

Motivation 5: Self-centred materialism.
Motivation 1: Intellectualization.

	5	1
77. I believe only in the triumph of the human spirit, and not in God.	+59	+17
34. The Christian faith is primarily something for the weak and helpless, children and old people.	+49	+18
73. God is only a construct of the mind made in the face of the finality and inevitability of death.	+46	+18
122. The meaning of life consists in getting on in one's occupation.	+30	+46
123. The meaning of life consists in acquiring the widest possible knowledge.	+21	+55
124. The meaning of life consists in acquiring the best possible and most extensive education.	+4	+60
125. The meaning of life consists in doing something which is valuable not only for myself, but also for other people.	−5	+43

95. The thought of death compels me to live my life so
that when I die, everything will be in order. −20 +40
24. The man who has never learnt that human life
acquires its value in devotion to others, does not
know the true meaning of life. −41 +22
58. I believe that Christ desires the true happiness of
all men. −47 +18

It is true that in a past era, it was within the personal and private
sphere of the middle classes that faith came to be understood afresh and
acquired new power, but today the opposite is the case. The motivation of self-identification with the limited world of personal experience
is the strongest support for self-centred materialism and its open rejection of faith. Therefore orientation towards only 'private experiences'
proves something more than just indifference to that comprehensive
reality with which faith is concerned. Both motives coalesce in the fact
that the individual attributes significance only to what is closest to
him. The objective circumstances of the world outside and the call to
involvement in them are less and less present to the consciousness. One
feels that there is no support to be found either in extended circles of
experience or in trusting the people around one. Self-centred materialism aggravates the situation only in so far as the lack of security extends
in this case also to very close human relationships and to every kind of
common conviction. Accordingly the statements of faith which the
individual is able to adopt in either case still vary; self-centred materialism involves denial of belief in God, whereas identification restricted
to experiences around one's own person desires to retain belief in God
as an ultimate authority of creation and as a background to existence.

Motivation 5: Self-centred materialism.
Motivation 3: Identification restricted to experiences around
one's own person.

	5	3
77. I believe only in the triumph of the human spirit, and not in God.	+59	0
120. The meaning of life consists of having one day a lot of money.	+58	+18
2. My motto is: 'Live your life to the full, for after death there is nothing'.	+48	+33
112. I can best fight against fear by trusting to my strength, my ability and my luck.	+17	+39
3. I don't worry about the hereafter; I just do my best to do my duty in my occupation and towards my family.	+17	+42
71. I find confirmation of God's existence in the rule of nature, not in the Christian faith.	+2	+53

Opposition to the attitude of faith thus arises from various motivations. The attitude of opportunism, and the inevitable question about

what one can understand with regard to faith, reveal that un-
questioning acceptance of faith and relations with the wider aspects of
life has been exploded. In spite of diffuse fear and insecurity, men find
a solution in this situation by replacing faith with rationalizing considerations that get their subject-matter from a facile criticism of
religion. Death, the transitoriness of life and fear are regarded as
everyday problems common to all life. They no longer pose vital
questions challenging the individual in an intensive and personal way.
Now it is customary to define the relevance of faith thus: only that
conviction can be accepted and advocated which fits into one's preoccupation with the limited spheres of personal experience and which
serves to provide fulfilment there. This attitude receives a clearer basis
in the affirmation of the autonomy of the individual as exemplified in
self-centred materialism. Although the individual in today's society is
in fact dependent on his fellow-men to an extent never known hitherto,
he strongly refuses to commit himself in wider spheres of life or to put
trust in them. As these motivations meet, the limit is reached where
the contents of Christian belief can no more be incorporated in actual
behaviour.

To conclude, the attitude of faith is confronted with a strong counter-
position not only outside the ranks of nominal church members, but
also within the Church itself. The motives which contribute to this
counterposition by no means reveal only a lack of commitment or
indifference to faith. They clearly arise from sources which explicitly
reject the attitude of faith, and exclude consent to the formulations of
the Christian creed. Moreover these motives do not appear in a vague
or fluctuating manner, but are embedded in distinctive psychic
mechanisms which are in large measure taken for granted by contemporary man. Finally there is also present a clear inclination to
ponder over themes such as the meaning of life, transitoriness, death,
and love of one's neighbour with an understanding which is no longer
Christian, and to come to terms with them by means of convictions
formulated from a different point of view. If this were not so, it would
not have been possible to approach the problem with statements, that
is, credal affirmations, and through this to show the various motivations. Although these motives and their effects were described in
socio-psychological terms, one cannot deny them the quality of genuine
convictions. They have a great intensity and are therefore able to
launch their own credos.

(k) *The specific attitude of faith: loss and gain*

In the total structure presented by the various motivations, the
attitude of faith occupies an isolated position. None of the other basic
motivations contributes essentially to the attitude of faith. This picture
is merely the reverse of the tendencies previously described, and may
disclose the weakness of faith in a Church which comprises a large
majority of the population. But it leads one also to consider whether
the isolation of the attitude of faith is not an essential condition for

people to be able, under the influence of other pressures, still to have an approximate idea of what the decisive content of faith really is. If, for example, the attitude of faith were mixed up with opportunism or with feelings of anxiety or uncertainty, an attitude for or against faith would immediately be linked up partly with social conditions, partly with faith, partly with a recognition of helplessness and partly with the confession of belief. It would be less easy to grasp what constitutes the attitude of faith or why the Christian confession has to be rejected. The isolation of the attitude of faith from other socio-psychological motivations guarantees to a certain degree that, within the whole field of concern with basic questions of life, this aspect stands out sharply and is therefore also present in the other attitudes by denial or limitation.

(1) *Clarity through the conflict of motivations*

In the sphere of general Christianity, the Church cannot carry out her task of information and proclamation by attempting to integrate as large a bundle of supplementary motivations as possible into the attitude of faith. Examples of such an attempt are seen when, in the situation where general Christianity is found, the Church makes an approach to opportunism by emphasizing the Christian foundations of society; when it offers a psychological security in place of general anxiety; when, speaking 'as man to man', the Church adapts its proclamation to the narrow world of experience around the person. This kind of experimenting with belief, by attempting to shore up the attitude of faith with other motivations, can only, in today's situation, cause more confusion. Whatever may be the degree of detachment or rejection, there always exists a fundamental sense of what constitutes the reality of faith, and what the 'ability' to believe looks like. The Church, with its information, cannot avoid and skirt the conflict which men themselves feel between faith and their own ideas. It makes a real impact on general Christianity with its proclamation and information when it addresses itself to the frontier where that conflict is taking place, and fosters the awareness that faith is something quite different from other kinds of motivation. It is important here to notice that the understanding given to the attitude of faith is expressed in very direct and elementary terms. Regard for different theological interpretations, or reflections upon demands which are on too high a level, are both alike unknown to it.

On the one hand, willingness for self-sacrifice and devotion is a controversial point. Faith breaks through barriers to one's neighbour, to those who depend on one, and to all men, and meets God and his love within this break-through. This basic pattern of faith is understood and rejected. A person is not prepared to risk bestowing trust in order to receive trust, or to lose himself in service in order to discover his fellowship with others. It is here that the self-centred materialistic attitude comes into conflict with the attitude of faith. But people also have difficulties because they are ruled by a general feeling of

8

uncertainty, because they surrender to rationalizing deliberations, or because they wish to limit themselves to the small sphere of their own personal world of experience.

Motivation 5: Self-centred Materialism.
Motivation 6: Attitude of Faith.

	5	6
24. The man who has never learnt that human life acquires its value in devotion to others, does not know the true meaning of life.	−41	+35
17. How I am to God is shown in how I am to those people who are entrusted to me.	−41	+49
58. I believe that Christ desires the true happiness of all men.	−47	+62
60. I believe that Jesus Christ desires the true happiness of all men. This begins here and now, when he makes men capable of being fair to others and dealing honestly with them.	−33	+70
104. The only power that overcomes even death is the love of God.	−24	+79

On the other hand, there is opposition to the objectivity and reality in which the attitude of faith puts its trust. The conflict arises here over commitments which transcend the sphere of narrow and everyday interests. The attitude of faith is founded on testimony to a reality which extends beyond one's own sphere of existence—which in fact upholds the individual's existence. The possibility of accepting such a reality for oneself is related to an openness to the wider aspects of life and to the will to internalize them. Turning to a more comprehensive objectivity conflicts with the attitude of mind wherein a person is concerned to build up security for himself only in his occupation, his family and his intimate circle. At the same time, a blockage in the ability to get involved in a reality outside the personal sphere occurs if superficial opportunism prevents the search for reality, or if rationalizing deliberations cause one to explain away all broader convictions as mere 'ideology'.

Motivation 3: Identification restricted to experiences around one's own person.
Motivation 6: Attitude of Faith.

	3	6
22. The well-being of the community to which I belong is of more value to me than my own life.	−31	+27
118. I have no fear, because I believe in the immortality of my soul.	−48	+50
117. I have no fear, because I trust in God.	−38	+58
23. I would risk my own life for faith in Jesus Christ.	−40	+58

35. The Christian faith gives me security at all times.   −33 +66
78. I believe that I can understand my tasks and
opportunities to their full extent only if I understand them as a challenge and a promise from God.   −25 +75
12. Earthly life is only a stage on the way to eternal life.   −26 +80
64. Jesus is the resurrection and the life; he who
believes in him will live, even if he dies. And he
who believes in him in this life will not die in
eternity.   −17 +85

These conflicts cause the attitude of faith to be present also where
the other motives exist and to co-determine the situation. The likelihood that the attitude of faith may be present depends ultimately
on whether, in the other attitudes, there is still a conscious opposition
to an understanding that includes personal involvement and to trust in
a more inclusive reality.

(m) *Knowledge as a challenge to criticism of faith*

The distinctness of the attitude of faith among the various views is
important. But one must not overlook the other fact that there is a
general rejection of devotion to others and of concern for the broader
reality, both of which are associated with faith. The emphasis laid on
these sources of irritation may make it possible, for the time being, for
those who already believe to maintain the position of faith, but it
does not encourage others to seek access to belief. The challenge of
faith is alive, but there is no evidence of any positive desire to adopt
such an attitude.

The process of intellectualization only in part supports the attitude of
faith. It is the necessity of deliberation and of thinking through the issues
which divides motivations from one another. Intellectualization normally takes the extreme course whereby people, when faced with the
consequences of reflection, immediately make every attempt to escape
from the challenge. They rely upon a wholesale criticism of belief and
religion, and arm themselves with arguments based upon this criticism.
In this situation, neither the question of faith nor the problem of
ordering the wider relationships of life in a meaningful way provides
any incentive to intellectualization. The body of thought contained in
the tradition of faith is dismissed because, it is said, there is no knowledge to be found in the Church. No attempt is made to penetrate
the more complex facts in the environment, because the individual
gives up in face of the many different kinds of events which impinge
upon him.

However, there is also a parallel, though weaker, tendency to use
such deliberations as a means to reach an understanding of order in
life. Here reflection undermines a point of view which is only oriented
towards one's own wishes and material needs. Appreciation of the fact
that one's situation is shared by others, and the consciousness that one
must do justice to one's fellow-men, produce a link with the attitudes

of self-giving and openness to wider circles of existence and faith (cf. p. 100).

If intellectualization can bring about this broadening of a person's horizon, the further question arises whether the task of general knowledge, as an admittedly superficial appropriation of insights from philosophy, anthropology, history, biology and natural sciences, must necessarily be merely to facilitate the transition from one's own reflections to a ready-made criticism of belief. Any increase in objective knowledge for man today only confirms the triumph of the human mind over belief in God, or proves that faith is only a prop for the weak. The results of progress in various fields of knowledge, which are seeping into the general consciousness, although in themselves matter-of-fact and indeed serving to broaden man's experience of the world, are nevertheless continuously used for just this type of criticism of belief. They hardly lead to man's acquiring a view of the broader aspects of life, or to an objective insight into the world outside his own limited experiences and immediate interests.

> Motivation 1: Intellectualization.
> Motivation 5: Self-centred Materialism.

		1	5
123.	The meaning of life consists in acquiring the widest possible knowledge.	+65	+21
80.	Man is not created by God, but is merely the product of a purely biological process.	+32	+35
5.	I live on only in my life's work and in my family, not in the hereafter.	+25	+25
33.	The Christian faith arose historically and will disappear historically.	+19	+31
73.	God is only a construct of the mind made in the face of the finality and inevitability of death.	+17	+43
34.	The Christian faith is primarily something for the weak and helpless, children and old people.	+18	+49
77.	I believe only in the triumph of the human spirit, and not in God.	+17	+59

Of all the basic motivations, for the attitude of faith it is of the utmost importance that the general feeling of doubt whether it is possible to know or grasp anything should be removed. Knowledge and understanding, even in their most general form, can bring light to bear on a person's own experience and views. Knowledge helps the individual to open up the context of his existence and to bring wider spheres of life into relation with his own position. Moreover, it must be added that a willingness to ask, to recognize and to know also provides a motive for the attitude of faith itself. It is of decisive importance to strengthen this independent sphere of knowledge which reaches out to the various departments of an individual's life. The critical attitude to faith, which usually saps away immediately the strength of such impulses and is satisfied with ready-made judgments, would become much more questionable. For there is little possibility of reconciling a willingness to broaden one's understanding with the process of quickly converting experiences into ready-made solutions that criticize faith. If the acquisition of new knowledge and its related arguments often serves only to heighten the self-centred materialistic point of view and the individual's limited concern for his personal affairs, it is necessary to rehabilitate the intrinsic worth of knowledge and its function in assisting in orientation.

For today's public, any downgrading or subordination of knowledge to faith will serve only to consolidate the present situation. Just as the Church explains generally-held opinions to the Christian by dismissing them as beside the point, or blurs their contours within a Christian '*Weltanschauung*', so men feel justified in exploiting knowledge for what is in their eyes a better purpose, using it for their personal argumentation against faith. They find confirmation for themselves in the process of not applying general insights in accordance with their specific intention (and with their help seeking to find their own place in the wider spheres of life) but of bending such knowledge to fit their own purpose and using it as a justification of their narrow opposition to belief. The attitude of faith ought to demonstrate that it does not feel itself threatened by knowledge and understanding, but that faith also lives and grows from the same roots and motivations. There is then room for a growth in understanding of the fact that, in approaching the basic questions about life, the task of knowledge need not be limited to a denial of belief.

The offering of knowledge is one of those things which today often serve only to heighten the individual's feeling of uncertainty and his impression that his environment is making exorbitant demands on him. A general offer of this kind only adds to the numerous influences which are impinging on the individual, with which he can no longer come to terms. Such procedures serve rather to make it more difficult for him to involve himself trustfully in the wider aspects of life. Because of this, the Church's efforts to support the intrinsic significance of knowledge, in contrast to the ready-made slogans of a critical attitude to belief, can be initiated only within the sphere of an individual's private and personal experience. The indications are that the Church must move away from the sphere of public activity, back to the people who are members of the local church, who express their faith in their occupations, their families and their personal decisions. Where they meet, proof must be furnished whether or not the attitude of faith is only a narrow view, withdrawn into the realm of personal experience and shut off from other spheres of existence. A narrow attitude of faith in the long run evokes a similarly narrow form of criticism. On the other hand, an attitude of belief which is inspired by the desire to understand and comprehend will be met by a type of criticism which is itself obliged to practise an understanding and comprehension of the broader aspects of existence.

If the passionate conviction of faith is to be conveyed, there are two conditions which must be met in the situation where general Christianity is found. The attitude of faith must be clearly distinguishable from other motivations, and belief as well as unbelief must enter into the debate concerning the recognition and ordering of the broader relationships in life. Otherwise the attitude of superficial resignation will continue to hold sway, as is exemplified in this remark of one of the respondents:

'You reach belief by the grace of God or through your own efforts and own decision. If you do not make it that way, you really have failed.'

CHAPTER 3

Witness in its Public Context

I. CONVERSATION ABOUT BELIEFS, WITH THE GENERAL PUBLIC AND
WITHIN THE CHURCH

(a) *Two communications circuits*

When people talk about their beliefs, there are today two different
circles of communication in which they can do so. In the one, the
participants in the discussion examine what is offered by the proclamation of the Gospel, as it is put forward by the Church. This is talk
about belief among the general public. In the other circle, the
participants discuss and criticize the usual understanding of faith and
Christian responsibility. This is talk about belief within the Church.
In both circles the Gospel is proclaimed, but in different ways. In the
first case, Christian assertions are introduced into a conversation and
must prove their strength in competition with other points of view. The
receiving of these statements constitutes the missionary movement
which occurs here. In the other case, the debate concerns the renewal
of Christian living and the Church, and the form that the missionary
awakening takes in this case is that, as a result of their strengthened
familiarity, and natural intimacy with the faith, men reach the point
of taking new paths and acting together.

Discussion which deals with Christian assertions compares the
Church's proclamation with the points of view and verdicts of other
spheres of influence and social institutions. This conversation is
carried on in public, because here people *question the content and importance of the faith, being impressed by other viewpoints and their social significance.*
In this form of communication of the faith, how typical is the making of
comparisons is shown by the detailed interviews with the persons
questioned and many of their statements of faith. The participants in
these conversations try to hear what is special in the message of
Christian belief. The most varied judgments upon the Church and the
faith result, depending on how people estimate the strength and
dynamic of other views. The common characteristic of public communication of the faith, however, is that all participants, no matter
what the degree of intensity with which they take part, want to be able
to grasp what constitutes the faith. The institutional basis for talk
about the faith in this form is supplied by the different levels of integra-
tion into global society, upon which modern public life in the abstract
is built. Here the Church and the faith stand alongside interests and
voices from other areas of life, and are commented on by people with
other points of view. Religious education has its place along with the

other school subjects; Christian writing represents one branch among others in literature; in the mass media the Church gets a word in edgeways alongside the other social institutions and interest groups, and in adult education Church and Faith constitute one subject for discussion along with others. In addition, people make a special claim on the Church for the private, family occasions of birth, majority, marriage and death, so that the Church and Christian belief appear to have competence in one particular area of life, while in the global society other organizations and establishments regulate other aspects of life. The co-existence of Christian influence with thoughts and attitudes streaming in from other directions compels one to question the particular Christian assertions. The rational methods of argument in the exploratory interviews, and the strength of the rationalizing attitude, revealed how prevalent is the compulsion to ponder over things.

Even though talk about the renewal of the Church and Christian life receives widespread attention today, it still takes the form of a discussion internal to an institution. It proceeds by setting forth the great significance of the confession and faith, and brings up the question, *what does faith mean today, and, in the present situation, what consequences follow from it both for conducting one's own life and for the tasks of the Church and congregation?* Ideally speaking, the participants in this conversation are in favour of belief and convinced of the necessity to understand afresh and more deeply what it is all about. They may enter the discussion from widely separate points of departure, and the discussion is thus not completely devoid of tension. But it is held together by a common concern for Christian belief and a readiness to re-examine its importance. The focal points of such discussions within the institution are sermons and conversations about them, also discussion in local church groups, and the communication which takes place through the extra-parochial work of the Church in connection with social service, welfare work, youth work, and so on. In the communications circuit within the institution, a large number of opinions are formed and questioning is very intense. Nevertheless only a small number of people are involved in this intense conversation.

For the Church, it is not a new situation that proclamation operates both in public conversation on the subject of faith and at the same time in discussions within the institution. The difference between the Church's service to its nominal members and its congregational work shows indeed that this state of affairs is recognized. To an increasing extent the Church has tried to take account of the way in which proclamation should take place in one or other of these communications circuits. In doing so, those with biased opinions may easily prevail by using theological arguments which give priority to one of these types of conversation, with the result that true proclamation is thought to have its place either among the general public only or in the Christian community only. People forget that each of the two circuits has its own group of hearers, who bring their own hypotheses into the conversation, pose their particular questions, and realize that they are influenced in their reflections by a particular social setting. The structures of these conversations vary, so as to correspond not only with distinct approaches to faith but also with very real social conditions. Identification with the congregation, for example, is for many people a hindrance to understanding the faith, surmountable only with very great difficulty.

(b) Proclamation in public discussion

Study of the situation among nominal Christians has shown two things. First, people today find themselves in an embarrassing situation in regard to belief. They know that they are not well informed in matters relating to belief; they therefore push aside the problem of how to reach a clear conviction and a firm attitude regarding the faith. On the other hand, other very powerful basic attitudes stand in opposition to the attitude of faith, and these tend to drive out even the wish for security in belief. In its place they offer an opportunism, a confining of oneself to one's personal world of experience or a materialism which excludes everything else. Although other ideologies have little to offer in comparison with Christian conviction, yet on the level of real motives, Christian belief is sharply disputed. These other basic attitudes influence the disappearing remnants of knowledge of the faith and draw them into their wake, so that men find it increasingly difficult to grasp what faith means. The detached way of considering things, the turning to personal affairs, and the mistrust of everything that goes beyond the immediately useful, prevent people from arriving at that state of confidence and objectivity which affords the basis for being a Christian. Nevertheless, all this does not mean that the search for faith has been completely submerged.

As a rule, proclamation in public discussion emphasizes Christian responsibility for the world and its relevance to current problems. In fact, the great themes of death and fear no longer move men. They are so very conscious of the threat of death and grief that they regard these subjects as commonplace. Proclamation to the public underlines the fact that even a very small degree of firm Christian conviction is sufficient to enable one to accept responsibility based on faith. Faith is linked not so much with particular views which define its meaning for the whole of society, but with common action in face of the necessities of the present time. It is not personal conviction possessed by each person that is decisive, but faith is proved or denied in service to one's neighbour, in social problems, political decisions, a search for new forms of community, critical acquaintance with the modern view of life, tensions in the world of labour, bridge-building between the generations and their outlooks, and in membership of the congregation. Such conversation will be not about solemn things but everyday things, not about Sunday but events in the week, not about a person's inner life but one's fellow-men, and not about individuals but the congregation. In this way proclamation goes against the inclination to limit faith to an area of opinion which is separate from the daily needs and decisions of men.

But there is a limit to what can be done in the attempt to 'actualize' a person's existing positive attitude and to lead him to accept responsibility. Today alongside the Christian view are other basic attitudes which suggest to the individual just as complete a chain of motives as does faith. Thus the appeal to accept responsibility does not now touch the conscience, but starts up a very complex contest between basic attitudes that cannot be solved by reasoned arguments or through striving for insight. Our investigation has come up against such conflicting values in respect of the image of the Church, of relationship to the faith, and particularly of comparison of the attitude of believers with the tendency to a non-Christian religiosity. If the Church goes with the times, then people see it as an attempt to court them in order to win back its declining influence in society. The idea of sacrifice and active participation in wider relationships is often expressly rejected. Every appeal based on faith which is vaguely general and made without any particular motivation therefore awakens emotional counter-reactions.

In these changed conditions, the missionary task lies in not leaving men alone with this conflict of vague attitudes. When *the Church and its members openly formulate the specific assertions of faith in public dialogue, and provide information about the faith which clearly expresses these assertions,* then they assist in transforming today's insecure attitudes into clearer convictions. Only when he is able to distinguish between differing convictions can the individual get back his freedom of choice. It is obvious that at the same time a process will be started of bringing agreement between the Christian faith and tradition and the themes which men on their side regard as included in the faith. It is not enough to repeat the traditional form of Christian teaching. But it is up to the Church, as well as to the individual Christian, to begin the dialogue by bringing the content of the faith into conversation among the general public.

(c) *Proclamation in discussion within the Church*

The impression might be given that such an understanding of the missionary task in public discussion places less emphasis on the striving for truth and a correct exposition of faith today, than on clarity of expression. To make such a judgment, however, would be to ignore the very strong debate going on within the Church which is enquiring into the renewal of faith in a changed religious situation and into new modes of church life in changed social circumstances. A readiness is displayed on all sides to investigate afresh the significance of the faith in a changed world and altered social conditions. In respect of the liberating message of the Gospel, the old answers, now outstripped by new understanding, are doubted and a new certainty of purpose is sought in all the ecclesiastical traditional forms. In looking at this type of conversation one must call it an internal discussion, because only a limited number of people is involved. In the minds of nominal church members, the internal discussion lends colour to the image of the Church, insofar as it underlines the struggle for contemporaneity or shows an awareness that interpretation is necessary if proclamation is to take place. But the discussion within the Church produces no stimulus in basic attitudes for or against the Church. One essential result of the investigation is represented in the fact that internal debate in the Church is clearly separated from public discussion about faith.

In the search for renewal there is always criticism of existing convictions and established practices. The Church is therefore concerned lest, in the internal debate, this critical current might carry away the basis of Christian belief. It is afraid that a radical position, allied with public opinion, might lead to a falsification of the meaning of the faith and the Church. *Proclamation in the internal communications circuit, therefore, must lead to reflection upon the spiritual centre of the faith.* Problems as such must not be mentioned, but doubts must be overcome and the great answers of the Gospel put forward positively. Critical questions and doubts will then be understood to come from outside the Church and from a body of opinion which is forming in society against the faith. The problems created by the increase in general knowledge will indeed be raised in the discussion, but the Church's proclamation must reflect the basic Christian truths which have little in common with the technical-scientific horizons of the modern world. Those who want to call Christians to accept responsibility in social or political affairs have a chance to be heard in discussion. The special characteristic of the Church, however, must not be its action in society but solely the message committed to it. The thoughts which are decisive for faith from many areas of modern life rebound from an orientation towards the one foundation on which the creed stands and the Church is built. If among the public there is little understanding of the faith, then at least proclamation must bring the participants in this internal discussion to a deeper insight into the authority of the faith and the Church.

Proclamation through conversations about the renewal of faith must define its task differently if it takes the internal character of the debate seriously. Here are people talking together who are not in any danger of losing their faith, but who are interested members of the Church and possessors of a living faith. The fact that the participants share this common concern also prescribes the limits of the discussion. It is not justifiable to fear that an abundance of critical reflections might bring confusion about the Church's task, though this might happen among the general public. It is the desire for substantial and devoted discussion about religious matters on the part of a small section of church members which sustains the struggle for renewal. One should not identify this kind of discussion with the public debate, nor should it be encumbered by the argument that it is jeopardizing the public status of the Church. *Proclamation in the internal debate within the Church must indeed move forward into new areas of Christian life, in solidarity with the various social organizations,* and widen the outlook of faith as against a way of thinking which relates exclusively to the Church.

Although there is so little overlap between the public sphere of communication about belief and the discussion within the Church, nevertheless the debate about the renewal of the Christian way of life has an indirect connection with the uncertainty about faith among the population in general. Every increase in experience and knowledge presents a challenge to belief. When one encounters such new and wider experience, the faith must not only be maintained and declared, but its strength must be newly understood. Even if public recognition plays a part in the process by which the faith is newly comprehended, the challenge is essentially one that is directed to the individual. He must reach his own new appreciation of the faith and himself win through to a deeper experience of it. Therefore the members of the Church can individually help one another to attain this new understanding of the faith, while universally-expressed opinions about Christianity remain unavailing. In communication about the faith in public, people play off the growth of knowledge and experience against faith, and turn modern discernment against belief. Increased understanding does not simultaneously result in a positive attitude to wider and far-reaching relationships in living, on whose support the individual can rely. *Only the man who himself, because of his doubts and uncertainties, has questioned the faith anew can help another so to unfold the faith that it takes in this increased experience and knowledge.* The task of proclamation in the internal discussion lies in revealing afresh the certainty of the faith by means of critical questioning. Participation in this discussion gives a Christian the freedom to take into his certainty the uncertainty and criticism of other men.

Proclamation is conveyed by two movements: under God, to understand the world; and, before the world, to testify to God's lordship. In place of the inclination to exercise one's understanding in the public debate and to make one's testimony within the Church, the situation regarding general Christianity demands testimony in the course of public conversation, and new understanding in the internal discussion within the Church.

2. PATTERNS OF CHRISTIAN WITNESS AND THE PROCESS OF SECULARIZATION

(a) *Patterns of Christian witness and the social structure*

Our investigation encountered various forms of Christian witness. Each of these forms comprises a particular way of proclaiming the Gospel and making it effective among men. They are each adapted at any given time to a specific pattern of social structure.

The first form of witness can be described as the *transmission of personal convictions.* This form of witness is closely related to middle-class society and the private lives of the middle classes. Here people remember their parents' home, in which the parents lived an exemplary life of faith and made it real for their children. The things which men received from their parents in the family circle as they grew up became the foundation for the whole of their subsequent lives. In middle-class society, people met personalities in the parish who were generally respected and who combined a deep piety with their social influence and professional competence. These persons carried conviction, because in them general respect and an upright behaviour based on faith met. Public regard for them gave weight to their personal Christian conviction. But their Christian conviction made them react more humanely and with greater foresight in professional and public affairs. In middle-class society personal convictions made an impression, for the most important subject in life was the search for an independent, personal stance.

The preconditions for the transmitting of faith by personal conviction reached far into the social structure. As a protest against the authoritarian and hierarchical pattern of feudal society, a personal culture developed in middle-class households. The independent economy of the family made it possible for the middle classes to go their own way. Traditions were questioned in education, politics, the arts and in Christianity. Middle-class families subordinated social conventions to the search for truth and personal identity. Within this struggle to find an independent standpoint was included the search for a personal expression of faith. In local politics personal convictions were still not without importance. Middle-class families had carried through their claim to mould local political life, and this possibility of determining the fate of the community challenged them to adopt a committed and personal attitude. If Christian witness is understood as the transmission of personal convictions, the idea is bound up with the basic theme of middle-class society. Today, however, it must be noted that the awakening of middle-class society with its search for personal expression has itself in turn produced the conventions of middle-class culture.

The second form of witness which appeared in the investigation was *dialogue between faith and ideologies or social interests*. Witness to the faith in dialogue is bound up with the repoliticized social sphere of a developed industrial society, in which large social organizations create the pattern of opinions and conditions of private life. In addition to the faith and the Church, other comprehensive ideologies have appeared. The verdicts on belief, such as were employed in the investigation, show their influence very clearly. The Marxist traditions of thought inherited by the labour movement and freethinkers, for example, are contained in the following convictions: 'Men create history through their work, not God', 'Faith is something for the weak and helpless, children and old people', and 'Faith is only something to help make dying easier'. The belief in science belonging to an age of technology is upheld by the following verdicts: 'I believe only in the triumph of the human spirit, and not in God', 'The Christian faith is no help to anyone', 'Jesus is only a historical person', 'God is a construct of the mind', and 'Man is not created by God, but is merely the product of a purely biological process'. The idealism of the educational tradition speaks in the emphasis on values and religious feeling: 'The readiness to do something which is of value not just for oneself, but for all men', 'the good of the community', 'the fulfilment of one's duty', 'Christian tradition', 'God is seen in the rule of nature', and 'the joy of living'.

In these ideological positions it is always a question of the convictions which the individual shares with a large social group, such as members of the working class, 'modern' people, or educated people. Christian witness therefore is now directed to all social groups. It speaks to socialists and freethinkers when it says, 'God will restore justice and love to the divided world through Christ', or 'Christ desires the true happiness of all men'. For the modern positivists, Christian witness expresses what is concrete in faith: 'Jesus Christ is the man for all men, and through him God is made real to us.' Christian witness meets the idealist in that it emphasizes the great significance which devotion and self-sacrifice have for faith.

As Christian witness entered into this kind of dialogue with the ideologies, a further piece of evidence appeared. The ideological criticism of faith is only partly based on a personal and precisely understood conviction. It has just as great a foundation in the interests and influence of the great social organizations. The Church could not speak to the socialists and freethinkers of justice, love and fulfilment without itself adopting a social policy for those who lack freedom and are excluded from the general welfare. If it did not take a constructive part in social conflicts and problems, its witness would be worthless. Similarly in the eyes of the positivists and their trust in science, to base the faith on the humanity of Jesus Christ would remain an empty formula if the Church did not uphold Christian humanism in the debate with the specialized sciences, in the field of education and in public discussion. With the idealists, the Church could point to the value in devotion and sacrifice only if it were itself serving the outcastes, helpless and suffering.

For this reason, the dialogue between faith and the various ideologies changed into a *dialogue between the Church and the large organizations which represent social interests*. In the ideological criticism of belief, social interests and personal convictions were merged. In the same way Christian witness itself received a politico-social dimension. In the play of forces between the social organizations which to a large degree affect the opinions of the individual, faith itself proves to be one of the influences which help to create social reality. The contribution of faith to the future of society becomes an essential aspect of witness. In such a situation it is understandable that men regard the Church as a social organization, that the Church publicizes its service to society, and that in the opinion of church members it ought to advertise its contribution even more strongly.

The repoliticized social sphere of developed industrial society and witness in the form of dialogue create a unity. Development towards a repoliticized social sphere begins when increasingly large numbers of people adopt the middle-class way of life as a goal which society must enable the individual to attain. Society can respond to this claim only by creating large-scale social organizations. Security of living conditions, which in middle-class society was guaranteed for each family by its property, enterprise and ability, is now assured for the broad mass of the population by social institutions. They offer the economic security on which personal living standards are built. In the same way, society provides for its members the personal cultural standards which, in the middle-class era, had their foundation in a private, independent sphere of life. The social institutions provide the individual with the material out of which he produces his own ideals and convictions. Personal culture is propagated by society.

In the early stages of the repoliticization of social life, the dominating factors are the ascendancy of social interests and the conflict between ideologies. Here faith meets its ideological criticism, which Christian witness must face up to and answer. At a later stage, when the essential goals have been attained, the co-ordination of interests, the planning and advertising of institutional activities, and the appeal for co-operation in them, become the overriding problems. At this point the Church and its members must enter into dialogue with the social institutions which make far-reaching decisions affecting the people who are in their charge.

The third type of witness appears as a demand which arises in many parts of the investigation. Witness must take the form of *providing information about faith*. People increasingly feel themselves to be incapable of making a decision for or against faith or of conducting a dialogue with faith from an ideological standpoint. For very many people, faith and the Church are remote, beyond the borders of the subjects of which they have knowledge and on which they can express themselves. In the repoliticized social sphere a scepticism is spreading with regard to the large social institutions which initiated this development. The individual feels that the social institutions no longer embrace existing ideas and make them operative in society, but that they must of necessity to a certain extent be leading opinion and creating convictions. For the individual member of society there is small hope of checking this from the outside. In church circles this situation is evidenced from the fact that the church members' tendency is towards private religion. The relation of private religion to Christian faith is hazy, but this troubles the individual very little.

At the same time the social institutions do not wish to act only in the interests of special social groups. They emphasize their significance for the whole of society, and they speak to as wide a number of people as possible with their claims and traditions. In this way the dialogue between ideologies and social interests is brought to the attention of the individual, who is exposed to the propagandizing efforts of all these bodies. The various outlooks meet in the consciousness of the individual member of society and there create a loose and vaguely related collection of convictions. Outlooks which vary greatly and are even contradictory appear side by side and are meaningful for the individual. The debate about ideologies and social interests no longer

takes place so much between defined groups in society, but rather has
shifted directly into the conscious arguments and reflections of the
individual. Therefore witness which seeks to carry on a dialogue can
find partners only to a very limited extent in particular sections of the
population. If faith desires to speak with representatives of other attitudes, it will find itself being directed towards the conversation
between social institutions, in which the broad mass of the population
takes part only very indirectly.

In the present situation, in which society is determined by the social
organizations, everything depends on *bearing witness to the faith in such a
way that people can deal with it themselves.* Christian witnesses must tell
what they know. Faith will not so much be accepted on the basis of the
personal conviction of those who pass it on—in a mobile and spacious
society, usually one can no longer see how anyone maintains his convictions amid the conflicts and problems of daily living—rather, people
ask what is the content of faith, apart from the personal experience and
life-history of the witness, which the questioner has not shared. People
do not wish to exchange one form of private religion for another, but
desire to receive information about the comprehensive ground of faith.
They expect a witness which neither simply repeats the Christian tradition and teaching, nor one which simply points to subjective decisions.
The kind of witness which provides information about faith is rather
that which starts by being subjective and related to a particular
situation, but then leaves that behind. It speaks of the facts of the faith,
such as God, atonement, resurrection, hope and sacrifice, which go
beyond the realm of a personal decision for or against a traditional
Christian teaching or the realm of subjective convictions. Witness
which provides information does not speak of how a person leads a
Christian life, or how one can believe at the present day. It makes every
effort to say how faith is really oriented, beyond any limits imposed by
one's own way of life and the general situation. The advance into the
objectivity of proclamation makes belief acceptable, so that people can
themselves begin to turn it over in their minds. Then faith no longer
represents convictions which either come down to the present through
Christian tradition, or are represented by one or other of one's acquaintances, or appertain to the opinion of the Church. It says something
about reality and things as they are. With this kind of information,
people are given back their freedom to decide whether to reject these
things or to incorporate them in their own lives.

At the same time information about faith must be *specialist and even
biased.* Among the various outlooks of which people today are conscious
and that have significance for them in a vague way, the basis for faith
must be strengthened. In the face of this task, witness in the form of
dialogue involving discussion with other viewpoints, produces confusion. It may persuade the enquirer, but takes away from him the
possibility that he himself should weigh differing viewpoints against one
another. Witness in the form of dialogue presupposes that the other
person already possesses a firm conviction which can be changed in the

confrontation with belief. In the situation in which society is determined by the social organizations, however, such firm convictions are indeed rare. Witness in the form of dialogue therefore merely transmits a hazy picture of the faith mixed with other viewpoints. Witness encounters, not a desire for discussion, but an expectation of gaining some specialized knowledge of faith which will make it possible better to solve the questions and elucidate the reflections already in mind. Since people are themselves already standing on the borders between these various viewpoints, they feel that witness which simply once again reflects their present situation is not a help. A single-minded or even biased witness, on the other hand, provides the incentive to try to reach an opinion for oneself. It makes apparent the necessity for the individual to arrive at an orderly pattern in his accumulation of viewpoints and opinions. The one-sidedness of the information provided does not mean that witness can dispense with making an overture to the other person's position. The person who witnesses must listen to the other man as a partner, and share his situation and his questions. The act of witnessing does not speak about this process of understanding, but about the certainty which through it can be seized afresh.

(b) *Social effects of secularization*

The various forms of witness which became evident in the investigation represent reactions to the process of secularization in society. They must not be confused with positions in the theological discussion about the phenomenon of secularization. They illustrate, however, the social effect which secularization has had upon affiliation to the Church and upon people's understanding of faith. The changes in the form of witness show the direction in which secularization has influenced faith and religious experience among the broad mass of the population.

It can at once be clearly seen how middle-class society breaks down the unity of social and religious norms. Whereas in the feudal social structure, obedience to authority, the control of economic events by the ruling classes, and Christianity were inseparably bound together, within middle-class society a *liberation takes place leading to individual responsibility*. The ideal of personal direction of one's life takes the place of the traditional total world-view which was founded on religion. But middle-class ideals cannot be imagined without a fundamental willingness to question social traditions and to examine their worth in relation to individual goals. It was for this reason that belief lost its power of attraction either as custom or as a generally recognized system of teaching. In the form of personal conviction, however, faith comes close to the newly-discovered sense of individual responsibility. The decrease in church attendance, coupled with interest in Christian teaching, shows how deeply this transformation of Christianity into a faith which one can personally advocate has altered relations to the Church. The national Church is changing into a confessing community and a broadly-based Christianity is being reduced to the loyalty to the Church of a minority of the population.

9

The process of secularization is not just happening in Christian countries, but touches the whole world today. The great non-Christian religions, just like Christianity for the West, have provided a total interpretation of the world for their own spheres of cultural influence, closely allied with the political organization and social hierarchy which shape industrial life. The political, social and religious community used to coincide. The development of the modern State, the sources of industry newly opened up by technology, and the greater mobility of the population have together destroyed this unity. As in the West, for the non-Christian religions also the result of the confrontation with secularization has been a widespread decline in religious observance and in familiarity with the religious heritage of the past. Just as people in Europe speak of a 'post-Christian' era, one can, for example, speak of a 'post-Buddhist era' in certain countries of East Asia which have made considerable advances in their modernization.

Secularization sets men free to fashion their own lives. In consequence, it is possible to observe that distinguishable groups are forming of particular religious communities among the non-Christian religions. In these, traditional religious behaviour is assuming the form of a personal religious conviction. As in Christian countries, the decline in religious observance among the population in general is counterbalanced by an intense religious devotion, allied to individual responsibility, among smaller groups. This development, of which many examples can be found, has been described as the 'renaissance' of the non-Christian religions, with the advance of secularization.

In the second stage, the guiding principles of middle-class society spread throughout the whole population. In this stage the large-scale social organizations assume responsibility for assuring economic conditions and for propagating middle-class values. The individualistic character of responsibility, both in the field of local politics and in discussion among a limited number of economically independent families, has disappeared. In its place there has developed a *plurality of ideological and social interests*. Each of them emphasizes its importance both for the individual and for the general good of society. The multiplicity of interpretations brings about the collapse of the idea of a metaphysically-based order of things, and leads to an understanding of responsibility from a historical viewpoint. In theory the future will be open, and the values binding society together will begin to be seen as of relative worth. The aim of Christian witness in dialogue with the ideologies and social organizations is to lay common foundations which will do justice to the new shape of historical responsibility. The search for a common responsibility towards the future can be answered only by a dialogue between faith and other outlooks and interests. The Church becomes a partner along with the rest of the social organizations and, as such, receives attention from the whole of society, outside the circle of its active members.

A plurality of ideologies and social interests today has also gripped the countries in which non-Christian religions dominate the whole of social life. These countries are planning on a broad scale, in an attempt to reach in the shortest possible time a middle-class level of living conditions for their people. To do this, they must absorb the forms of social organization and the institutions of industrial society. However, along with the institutions, ideological elements and bodies which formulate social pressures also of necessity come into the country. These are the elements that have marked the development from the middle-class era to an advanced industrial society in Western countries. The tension between the traditional world and the process of modernization has undermined the strength of the religious systems. The plurality of convictions and outlooks in these nations has an international character. Consequently the relativization of binding values is more far-reaching, and the need to reach a new common ethos in keeping with future tasks is more pressing, than in Christian countries. The recognition of historical responsibility towards the future is often even more radical than in the West. For the non-Christian religions, this situation means that in them also political pressure is growing. In the modernization process they ally themselves with the struggles of nationalist, conservative or reforming groups. They open themselves to political debate and contribute to the building of the new society. In this way religion forms one of the spheres of political power in a country.

When one surveys these world-wide developments, one can easily come to the conclusion that the inherited forms of Christian and of non-Christian religion all over the world today face the same crisis. The world-wide process of secularization creates for Christian witness a similar point of departure in more or less all countries. It is produced by the spread of an individualist culture oriented towards material goals, which threatens religious observance and permits only a small minority of the population still to measure up to religious norms. It is characterized by the collapse of metaphysical thought and the release of the world from enchantment, features which take from traditional religion its pre-eminent position in the cultural heritage and place it in competition with the other social organizations. This point of departure represents the opportunity and the challenge facing Christian witness today throughout the world.

Such a manner of thinking, however, leaves out of account the large part of the population of any country which has given up traditional observances and can therefore usually be reckoned to follow the new, individualistic and materialist culture—in regard to the religious ideas of which, however, nothing is yet known. In the spectrum of opinions between rejection of religion and religious conviction and active participation, this part of the population is by far the largest group. It includes *all the people who no longer participate in the old forms of religious observance, but whose religious ideas have nevertheless not demonstrably altered.* It is among these people that one finds that secularization has the widest and the most effective influence, compared with all the rest of society. The present enquiry, which took place in the limited area of a German urban milieu, was directed towards the group of Christians who take no part in institutionalized religious life. The results enable one to formulate a theory about the social effects of secularization, the usefulness of which can be examined in the context of other religious traditions and other social conditions.

Secularization does not bring about the end of religion or of Christianity, and its replacement by a completely worldly outlook. Rather it leads to *a loose co-existence of the most varied viewpoints in men's consciousness. This loose juxtaposition of ideas includes the religious attitudes inherited from the past.* Among the multiplicity of viewpoints having little connection with one another, man is still on the alert in his search for truth, the meaning of life, and hope. This search takes place within the framework of the known inheritance of religious belief, Christian or non-Christian. People see themselves unable to solve the open questions because they lack the necessary knowledge to arrive at basic opinions in the field of religion. The inherited patterns in which religious convictions or Christian faith have been handed down have been rendered largely powerless by social change. When the Church or the non-Christian religious communities come to the fore as social organizations, the individual feels a wide distance between himself and official religion. This feeling of detachment leads to the tendency to shut oneself up in a materialist and 'privatistic' attitude to life, or to ally oneself to a popular religion (*Volksreligion*) which has no relationships outside the narrow confines of personal existence. Effective information about religion and faith, however, can also so strengthen the loose and uncommitted religious outlooks that the individual becomes capable of making well-founded decisions in his search for religion.

There are certain assumptions about the process of secularization which may become doubtful in the following up of this hypothesis. In Christian countries secularization does not yet mean that Christian outlooks have lost their influence in the population at large, or that Christian faith has become the affair of a small minority. It is not a fact that the small host of Christians are faced with the elementary task of understanding afresh God's presence in the upsurge of a secular age. Nor are the other great religions totally supplanted by secularization and modern social structures. They have not given way to a sense of loss of direction, or to the search for a new foothold, both of which, in the non-Christian lands, would demand the creative answer of faith to an unimagined degree. Rather the signs point to the fact that the confrontation of faith with non-Christian religions and outlooks on life is just beginning.

Decisions in this confrontation occur at the level of *popular religious ideas*, which are quite different from the fully-developed world of ideas of past generations. Theological dialogue between the official representatives of the religions, therefore, or a comparison based on the history of religions, is unable to achieve much in this debate. Similarly the confrontation with non-Christian views of life occurs on the level of everyday philosophy or general knowledge. The debate is not solved through discussion between theology and philosophical models or socio-philosophical systems. If Christian faith is to stand the test of confrontation with non-Christian religions and attitudes to life, this depends on two circumstances. First, witness must rid itself of the tendency to judge religion only by the degree of resultant participation in community activities and groupings, while overlooking the significance of religious ideas and the content of faith. Social change has permitted religious observance and the concept of the religious community to become matters of controversy. It is therefore important to understand faith from the angle of men's decisions and expectations. The other assumption is that witness must develop a solidarity of sympathy with popular belief. It rests not only on illiteracy, but also on the fact that the official importance of religious traditions and the authority of social organizations stifle the individual's own answers to religious questions. If witness desires in a responsible way to achieve a solidarity with popular belief, sympathy alone is insufficient to accomplish this. What is at stake is neither more nor less than bridging the gulf between the great tasks of the present time and the helplessness of the individual. Into this tension must be introduced man's witness to the mercy and justice of God.

Explanation of the Methods Employed

1. EXPLORATION

An exploration starts from the fact that frequently a person puts forward 'rational' grounds as an explanation for himself and others of particular ways of behaving or thinking. But these grounds do not always tally with the person's true motivations. In such a case the psychologist speaks of 'rationalization'. Certain factors are in part deliberately suppressed or in part driven into the subconscious.

The task of a psychological exploration is to recognize rationalizations as such, and to uncover as far as possible the layers of the conscious and unconscious motivations which lie behind them 'in depth'. With the help of a guide prepared in advance, the exploration proceeds in the form of a detailed, 'free' conversation (i.e. the respondent does not notice that he is being guided). Either the conversation is recorded on tape, or a written report is made, as nearly as possible word for word.

2. GROUP DISCUSSION

In this case also, as in the exploration, there is a free conversation, not noticeably guided, in which six to eight respondents take part with the discussion leader. In the course of it, the discussion leader opens up and plumbs thoroughly the whole subject matter of the question being investigated.

In addition to the depth aspect, these discussions are concerned with bringing to light and comprehending group aspects, such as strong or uncertain opinions; the general behaviour and ideas of the participants; changes of opinion; whether they are leaders of opinion or followers, etc. The conversations are tape-recorded and, in addition, the most important assertions and phases are minuted in shorthand.

3. ANALYSIS OF MEANING

An analysis of meaning is an exploration by the respondents into what they 'understand' by certain terms, how they explain them, what significance they attribute to these terms. The results are afterwards analysed and interpreted from a psychological point of view.

4. MEASUREMENT TECHNIQUES

The point of measurement techniques lies in drawing from the respondents' answers their ideas and motives in such a way that they are measurable and statistically calculable. For example, in the question-naire, in place of 'open' questions (in which the respondent's own answers are recorded), one uses 'closed' questions, in which a choice of several alternative answers is supplied. The psychologist's problem here is to compile a list of answers which will be as exhaustive as possible.

Rationalization is overcome in 'indirect' ways by using certain proved methods of association and role-playing (projective techniques), which offer the respondent the possibility of projecting towards other persons and things his own attitudes and motives. The attitudes are measured by a scale of, for example, o to 6, or −5 to o to +5, or by school marks 1 to 5, etc.

Measurement techniques also include the Attitude Statements method which was used in the main investigation. The statements are ready-made opinions to which the respondent must react in a pre-scribed way; in this case he had to answer either

I believe this;
I should like to believe this;
I cannot and will not believe this,
or I fully agree with this proposition;
I agree with this proposition, though with reservations;
I do not at all agree with this proposition.

The statements must correspond exactly with the subject matter and psychological structure, and at the same time be kept as simple as possible, so that they may be intelligible to the majority of respondents on the one hand, and on the other, as far as possible one-dimensional, i.e. expressing only one aspect of the attitude in question.

By means of lengthy preliminary tests, out of an original 250 state-ments, 111 were chosen for the main investigation, and these were then used in all phases of the collection and evaluation of evidence.

5. EVALUATION

Evaluation is the processing of the evidence by scientific methods, so as to arrive at an interpretation. It proceeds according to a classifica-tion into categories and sub-categories based on logic and psychology, and by drawing together facts and data which thematically and psycho-logically belong together, complement one another and are inter-locking. The interpretation proceeds according to psychological and sociological models which have been produced by study and experiment and verified in practice. In the explorations and group discussions (see above), the type of procedure is such that the recognized fact is indeed displayed exactly according to its psychological and sociological importance, although it is hardly possible to make numerical estimates in order to back it up or illustrate it.

As measurement techniques have been used in the enquiry, it is possible, in addition to classifying and drawing together the material, to sort out in numerical form the results collected, and then to work out percentages, averages, correlations and further statistical analyses, specially developed in accordance with psychological and sociological theory. Interpretation proceeds, as with explorations and group discussions, in accordance with psychological and sociological models. One particular technique of evaluation and interpretation is factor analysis, which is described in the next paragraph.

6. FACTOR ANALYSIS

Factor analysis is a method of applied mathematics used in psychology to deal with complex masses of data. It was developed between 1900 and 1950 by the psychologists and mathematicians, C. Spearman and L. L. Thurstone.[1]

In our main investigation, 111 'questions' were used, in the form of ready-prepared statements developed, on the basis of psychological and theological viewpoints, in the course of an extensive series of introductory studies and preliminary tests. The respondents' answers were collected in such a way that they could be quantified and submitted to analytical computation. The expression of the answers in pure percentage terms for each of the 111 questions (or statements) produces a picture that is interesting in some instances, but looked at as a whole gives very unstructured results. The correlation between the individual questions cannot be seen. The field of play for interpretation, i.e. deciding which questions belong together in what patterns, is very broad. Factor analysis provides the technique that makes it possible to discover by analysis, from the correlations between a group of interrelated characteristics, the conditions that are common to them. In this particular case, it is possible to examine the question of motivation, along with the structure upon which it is based.

In the first stage of abstraction in the analysis, it is a matter of bringing together interrelated questions. As we are dealing *not* with a scientific *analysis of the questions*, but an *analysis of the reactions of the respondents to the questions*, it is not the intuition and experience of the interpreter that must decide which questions should be grouped together. The decision is left to the data, or finally to the type of reactions of the respondents. Those questions are grouped together where one can predict from the reaction of a person to one of the questions with 100% certainty his attitude to another question, after specific and error variance have been eliminated. (Variance is the square of the scattering, i.e. the mean quadratic deviation of the characteristics covered from the average; specific and error variance can arise in individual cases if, for example, the formulation of a question is embarrassing to the respondent and he therefore deliberately answers something else, or if he misunderstands the sense of a question and gives a random answer. A by-product of factor analysis is the correction for random answers and misleading specifics.)

[1] Cf. as introduction L. L. Thurstone: *Multiple Factor Analysis*, Chicago, 1947.

The scale used in this stage of abstraction is the correlation which can vary from $+1$ to 0 to -1, and by squaring is converted into a percentage of the predictability and expressed as a scale of association. Factor analysis makes it possible to select and classify interrelated attitude questions, according to the principle mentioned above (viz., that the choice is made through the given material, not from outside), by using the correlations existing between the questions. Thus the factors represent the common element, the common idea or the common structure which links them. The number of factors which result are no more and no less than are necessary for it to be possible to reconstruct from them all the reactions to all the questions by a simple (linear) combination, according to the basic formula for factor analysis:

$$S_{ij} = L_{j1}F_{1i} + L_{j2}F_{2i} + \ldots L_{jr}F_{ri}$$

i.e. the reaction S of a person i to a question j can be reconstructed by the loading L of the question j on the factor 1 (loading = putting weight on the factor) multiplied by the score of the person i on factor 1 (score = weight, assent) plus the loading L of the question j on the factor 2 multiplied by the score of the person i on factor 2 plus ... (and so on, up to the last factor, r).

Sometimes factors which are independent or not correlated appear to indicate a common element in the questions being analysed; in this case, however, they clearly refer to a common element of a broader and more general kind than would primarily be required for the set of questions being investigated. This phenomenon occurs when one is investigating in very specialized fields. Human desires, needs, anxieties and attitudes manifest themselves in the most widely varied spheres of life; in the present investigation, the sphere picked out is the 'religious sphere', which means that the factors are of a more general kind than is necessary for the present case. They represent the general psychological background of the reactions to religious questions. In the completed factor analysis, the specifically religious reactions appear in *sum vectors* which do not directly fit in with the more general psychological factors that determine the reactions, but are concentrated among them.

APPENDIX 2

Table of Statements

THE ORDER of statements in this table has no significance, because in the interrogation the different parts of the schedule were rotated. By this means it was possible to balance specific reactions of the respondents which might occur at the beginning or towards the end of the interview.

1. I don't worry about what might happen after my death, but take each day as it comes.

2. My motto is: 'Live your life to the full, for after death there is nothing'.

3. I do not worry about the hereafter; I just do my best to do my duty in my occupation and towards my family.

4. I believe in life in the hereafter.

5. I live on only in my life's work and in my family, not in the hereafter.

6. Above all, one should behave in such a way that after death one is remembered with respect.

7. I believe that God will judge me at the Last Day.

8. I must live my life on earth in such a way that I can look forward to judgment at the Last Day with confidence.

9. My conduct on earth has no effect on how I fare in the hereafter.

10. I achieve inner peace only by being right with God.

11. For me the essential thing is to live a life which is based on God's Word and the Christian faith.

12. Earthly life is only a stage on the way to eternal life.

13. I believe that eternal life begins right from the moment I receive my earthly life from God's hand.

14. Eternal life does not come only after death: it is absolute trust in God.

15. I don't think much of loving your neighbour. My attitude is, 'If you want a thing done, you must do it yourself'. No one else will help me.

16. The essential thing about loving your neighbour is that you earn something for yourself if you help others selflessly.

17. How I am to God is shown in how I am to those people who are entrusted to me.

18. One's attitude to one's neighbour must be determined by obedience to God. That is real love of one's neighbour.

19. Good deeds done to one's neighbour will be rewarded in the hereafter.

20. My own life is for me the highest good.

21. I would risk my life for the sake of my family.

22. The well-being of the community to which I belong is of more value to me than my own life.

23. I would risk my own life for faith in Jesus Christ.

24. The man who has never learnt that human life acquires its value in devotion to others, does not know the true meaning of life.

25. You are on your own; the Christian faith is no help to anyone.

26. The Church has failed to make the Christian message intelligible to men of our time or to bring it home to them.

27. I regard the Christian message, as offered by the Church today, as an inheritance from the past which offers no solution to the unrest which surrounds us today.

28. The sermon is intended only for the small circle of church people.

29. For me the sermon proclaims the power and love of God, and shows me the one and only truth, the Word of God.

30. I experience the sermon as a speech addressed to me personally in the name and authority of Christ.

31. In our day the sermon has become meaningless and insignificant.

32. The Christian faith is nothing more than a help to make dying easier.

33. The Christian faith arose historically and will disappear historically.

34. The Christian faith is primarily something for the weak and helpless, children and old people.

35. The Christian faith gives me security at all times.

36. Actually I think about the Christian faith only when I am in misfortune, and am looking for consolation and encouragement.

37. Everything is laid down by fate, and in this even the Christian faith is no help.

38. Baptism is a symbol of that proclamation by which Christ comes to rule over us.

39. Because I am baptized, I am assured of the fact that God loves me as I am.

40. Because I am baptized, there is a place for me in the hereafter.

41. I am glad I was baptized, because this means I can have a Christian burial. The idea of simply being put into the ground without a church ceremony is one I find unpleasant.

42. Only by baptism am I made a member of the communion of saints.

43. I consider church ceremonies an unnecessary custom without meaning.

44. I don't worry much about Christian belief, but one must have baptism, confirmation, church weddings and church burials, because they are the accepted thing in our culture.

45. I don't worry much about Christian belief, but one must have baptism, confirmation, church weddings and church burials, for if I do not observe these ceremonies, I have disregarded God, if He exists.

46. You should have your child baptized, because you thereby put it under the protection of the Almighty.

47. You should have your child baptized, so that it does not seem an outsider later on.

48. I do not have my child baptized, because I have no connection with the Christian faith.

49. I think baptism is an empty form, because the personal conviction of the child is not involved.

50. I believe in the immortality of the soul.

51. I do not believe in the immortality of the soul, because death shows me that everything is transitory.

52. I believe in the immortality of my soul, because the idea that one day all will be over is simply inconceivable.

53. If you believe in the immortality of the soul, then separation by death from those you love is not so hard.

54. I believe in the immortality of my soul, because it is rooted in the Christian faith.

55. I am a Christian, because this is natural according to tradition and custom.

56. I believe in Jesus Christ, because in his actions and words God Himself acts and speaks.

57. I believe in the power of Christ to forgive me all my sins irrevocably.

58. I believe that Christ desires the true happiness of all men.

59. I believe that at the end of time Christ will restore justice and love to this whole torn world.

60. I believe that Jesus Christ desires the true happiness of all men. This begins here and now, when he makes men capable of being fair to others and dealing honestly with them.

61. I believe in Jesus Christ, so that on the Last Day I may enter God's Kingdom.

62. I believe in Jesus Christ, so that things may go well for me on earth.

63. Jesus is God's Son; he is the man for us all; he takes our place, for he died for us on the cross.

64. Jesus is the resurrection and the life; he who believes in him will live, even if he dies. And he who believes in him in this life will not die in eternity.

65. What I have learnt about Jesus Christ is so vague and confusing that I don't know any more what to make of it.

66. I would like very much to believe in Jesus Christ and accept the Christian faith without reservation, but I cannot do so because constant hesitation and doubt prevent me.

67. I do not believe in Jesus Christ and the Christian faith, because thinking about it is meaningless and confusing.

68. Jesus is not the Son of God, but only a historical person.

69. Jesus is a symbol which sums up for me the breadth and depth of humanity.

70. In Jesus Christ I find confirmation of the fact that God exists.

71. I find confirmation of God's existence in the rule of nature, not in the Christian faith.

72. I find confirmation of the fact that God exists, not in the Christian faith, but in looking into the great works of art and science.

73. God is only a construct of the mind made in the face of the finality and inevitability of death.

74. Even without being a Christian I believe in the goodness of man.

75. I believe that it is men alone who by their work shape history, and not God.

76. Sometimes I have the feeling that I am powerless in the hand of fate, and that even God cannot help.

77. I believe only in the triumph of the human spirit, and not in God.

78. I believe that I can understand my tasks and opportunities to their full extent only if I understand them as a challenge and a promise from God.

79. Man is God's creature and God watches over him.

80. Man is not created by God, but is merely the product of a purely biological process.

81. Whether man believes in God or not, he is always subject to God's rule and judgment.

82. Living in today's world, one often has a feeling of gloomy fear.

83. Sometimes I am afraid of the future.

84. Sometimes I am afraid of growing old.

85. Sometimes I am afraid of sickness.

86. Sometimes I am afraid of death.

87. I always think about death, even when the end of my life is not threatening me in any way.

88. The thought of death is terrifying to me, for after death everything is finished.

89. The thought of death does not terrify me, because I believe in the immortality of the soul.

90. The thought of death does not terrify me, because my life is supported by hope in God.

91. Since I have only received life as a temporary gift from God, death has lost its power over me.

92. Man today is on intimate terms with death. Death has lost its power to terrify the individual.

93. It is only when I constantly realize that I must die that my life has significance, and I am clear in my own mind about the fulfilment as well as the meaninglessness of what I do.

94. My life is free from worry only when I put on one side the thought of death.

95. The thought of death compels me to live my life so that, when I die, everything will be in order.

96. The thought of death compels me to insure against all the consequences of my death (by effecting insurances, making savings, building a house, etc.).

97. The thought of death compels me to try some time or other to get right with God.

98. The thought of death compels me to make the best of every minute of my life.

99. The thought of the end of my life makes me so afraid that I put it well on one side.

100. It is not so much death which shows me that everything in life is transitory, as the realization that in many a situation I have missed something which is beyond recall, or done something wrong.

101. Unless you continually consider the transitoriness of the moment, you cannot lead a reasonable life.

102. If I had always to think about the transitoriness of the moment, I should lose all joy in life.

103. Christ broke the power of death through suffering it to the very end.

104. The only power that overcomes even death is the love of God.

105. Death is the end of all things.

106. There is no death in the absolute sense, for after death comes eternal life.

107. Death is God's right and power over his creatures.

108. Christ is the risen one, who takes us up into his resurrection. All that we can do, and all the powers at our disposal, are pious self-deception in the face of the power of death. We can be liberated from death only by Jesus Christ.

I can best fight against fear by:

109. —quietening it by diversion.

110. —trying to forget it in work.

111. —living a healthy and careful life.

112. —trusting to my strength, my ability and my luck.

113. —building up defences such as savings, life assurance, etc.

114. —by prayer.

115. —by listening to a sermon.

116. —by my trust in God.

I have no fear:

117. —because I trust in God.

118. —because I believe in the immortality of my soul.

The meaning of life consists in:

119. —doing one's best to lead a morally irreproachable life.

120. —having one day a lot of money.

121. —having experienced and savoured the taste of everything to the full.

122. —getting on in one's occupation.

123. —acquiring the widest possible knowledge.

124. —acquiring the best possible and most extensive education.

125. —doing something which is valuable not only for myself, but also for other people.

126. —being able to say at the end of one's life, 'I have attained all I wanted'.

127. —fulfilling the tasks which God gives me.

128. —doing one's best to be right with God.

Demographic Characteristics of the Respondents in the Formal Interrogation

THE PERCENTAGE of persons interviewed was:

	%
Men	44
Women	56
	100

		%
Ages of the respondents:	21–29 years old	24
	30–39 years old	24
	40–49 years old	14
	50–59 years old	29
	60–70 years old	9
		100

Occupations of the respondents (the occupation of the head of the household is given in the case of married women not engaged in any employment):

	%
Professions	10
Owners of businesses and self-employed persons	8
Civil servants	8
Salaried employees	38
Skilled and unskilled workers	18
Other employees	18
	100

		%
Marital status:	Single	20
	Married	62
	Widows and widowers	10
	Separated/divorced	8
		100

APPENDIX 4

Diagrams of the Factor-correlations

Motivation **6:** *Attitude of faith*

Motivation **5:** *Self-centred materialism and sum-vector*

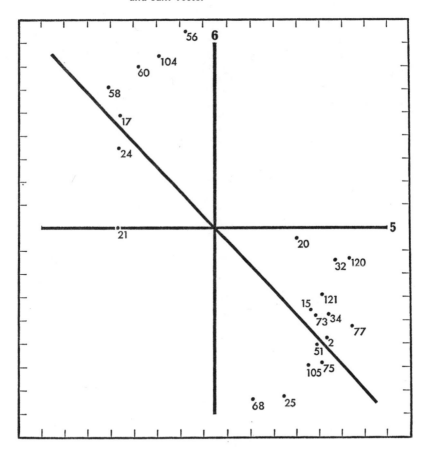

Motivation 6: *Attitude of faith*

Motivation 2: *General fear*

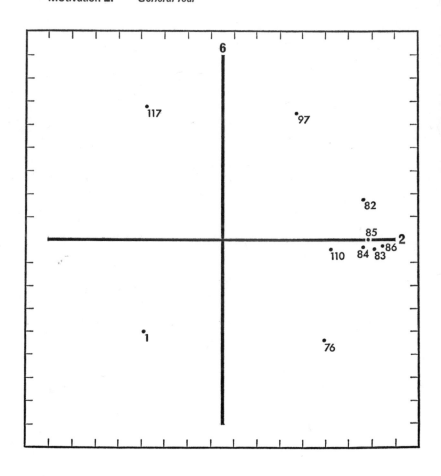

Motivation **6:**   *Attitude of faith*

Motivation **1:**   *Intellectualization*

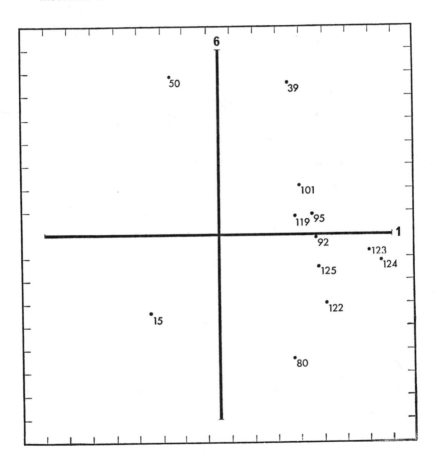

Motivation **5:**   *Self-centred materialism*

Motivation **1:**   *Intellectualization*

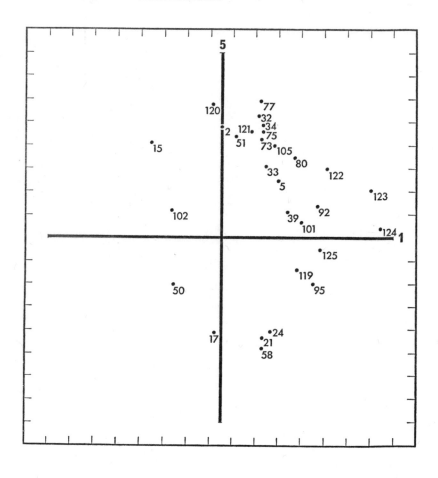

Motivation **6:**   *Attitude of faith*

Motivation **4:**   *Opportunism*

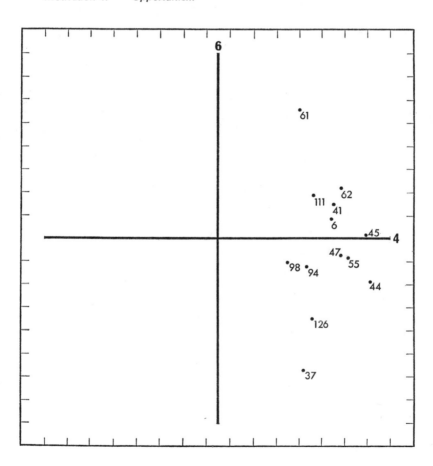

Motivation **6:**   *Attitude of faith*

Motivation **3:**   *Identification restricted to experiences*
                     around one's own person

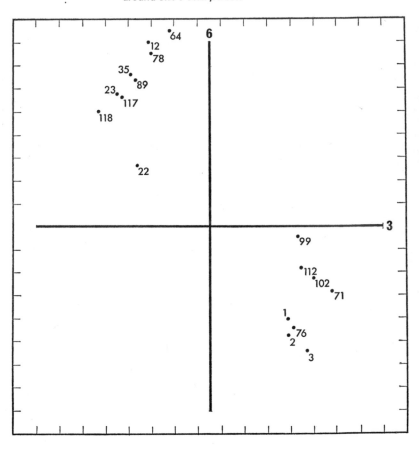

Motivation 5:   *Self-centred materialism*

Motivation 3:   *Identification restricted to experiences
around one's own person*

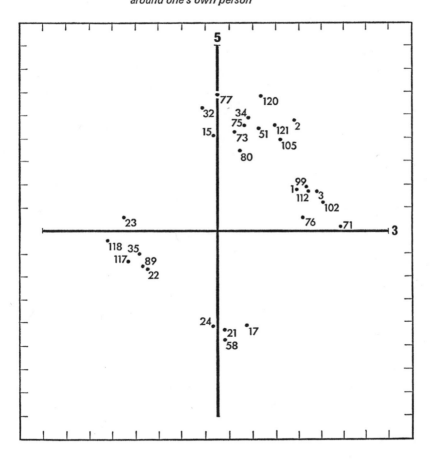

INDEX

World Studies of Churches in Mission

Published to date:

The Growth of the Church in Buganda: An Attempt at Understanding
by John V. Taylor, 1958, SCM Press, London.
Christians of the Copperbelt: The Growth of the Church in Northern
Rhodesia, *by John V. Taylor and Dorothea A. Lehmann, 1961, SCM
Press, London.*
A Church Between Colonial Powers: A Study of the Church in Togo,
by Hans W. Debrunner, 1965.
The Church as Christian Community: Three Studies of North Indian
Churches, *by J. P. Alter, H. Jai Singh, E. Y. Campbell, and Barbara
M. Boal (ed. V. E. W. Hayward), 1966.*
Urban Churches in Britain: A Question of Relevance, *by Kofi A. Busia,
1966.*
Stranger in the Land: A Study of the Church in Japan, *by Robert Lee,
1967.*
Solomon Islands Christianity: A Study in Growth and Obstruction,
by Alan R. Tippett, 1967.
Churches at the Grass-roots: A Study in Congo-Brazzaville, *by Efraim
Andersson, 1968.*
Village Christians and Hindu Culture: Study of a rural church in
Andhra Pradesh, *by P. Y. Luke and John Carman, 1968.*
Haven of the Masses: A Study of the Pentecostal Movement in Chile,
by Christian Lalive d'Epinay, 1969.
Sri and Christ: A Study of the Indigenous Church in East Java, *by
Philip van Akkeren, 1970.*

All the above except the first two have been published by
Lutterworth Press, London